SIXTH EDITION

INTERACTIONS 1

Listening/Speaking

Judith Tanka

Paul Most

McGraw Hill

Interactions 1 Listening/Speaking, Sixth Edition

Published by McGraw-Hill ESL/ELT, a business unit of The McGraw-Hill Companies, Inc.,
1221 Avenue of the Americas, New York, NY 10020. Copyright © 2014 by The McGraw-Hill
Companies, Inc. All rights reserved. Printed in the United States of America. Previous editions
© 2007, 2001, and 1995. No part of this publication may be reproduced or distributed in any
form or by any means, or stored in a database or retrieval system, without the prior written
consent of The McGraw-Hill Companies, Inc., including, but not limited to, in any network
or other electronic storage or transmission, or broadcast for distance learning.

Some ancillaries, including electronic and print components, may not be available to customers
outside the United States.

This book is printed on acid-free paper.

7 8 9 0 QVS/QVS 1 0 9 8 7 6 5

ISBN: 978-0-07-759518-0
MHID: 0-07-759518-1

Senior Vice President, Products & Markets: Kurt L. Strand
Vice President, General Manager, Products & Markets: Michael J. Ryan
Vice President, Content Production & Technology Services: Kimberly Meriwether David
Director of Development: Valerie Kelemen
Marketing Manager: Cambridge University Press
Lead Project Manager: Rick Hecker
Senior Buyer: Michael R. McCormick
Designer: Page2, LLC
Cover/Interior Designer: Page2, LLC
Senior Content Licensing Specialist: Keri Johnson
Manager, Digital Production: Janean A. Utley
Compositor: Page2, LLC
Printer: Quad/Graphics

Cover photo: foto76/Shutterstock.com

All credits appearing on page iv or at the end of the book are considered to be an extension
of the copyright page.

The Internet addresses listed in the text were accurate at the time of publication. The
inclusion of a website does not indicate an endorsement by the authors or McGraw-Hill, and
McGraw-Hill does not guarantee the accuracy of the information presented at these sites.

www.mhhe.com

www.elt.mcgraw-hill.com

The *McGraw·Hill* Companies

A Special Thank You

The Interactions/Mosaic Sixth Edition team wishes to thank our extended team: teachers, students, administrators, and teacher trainers, all of whom contributed invaluably to the making of this edition.

Maiko Berger, **Ritsumeikan Asia Pacific University**, Oita, Japan • Aaron Martinson, **Sejong Cyber University**, Seoul, Korea • Aisha Osman, Egypt • Amy Stotts, **Chubu University**, Aichi, Japan • Charles Copeland, **Dankook University**, Yongin City, Korea • Christen Savage, **University of Houston**, Texas, USA • Daniel Fitzgerald, **Metropolitan Community College**, Kansas, USA • Deborah Bollinger, **Aoyama Gakuin University**, Tokyo, Japan • Duane Fitzhugh, **Northern Virginia Community College**, Virginia, USA • Gregory Strong, **Aoyama Gakuin University**, Tokyo, Japan • James Blackwell, **Ritsumeikan Asia Pacific University**, Oita, Japan • Janet Harclerode, **Santa Monica College**, California, USA • Jinyoung Hong, **Sogang University**, Seoul, Korea • Lakkana Chaisaklert, **Rajamangala University of Technology Krung Thep**, Bangkok, Thailand • Lee Wonhee, **Sogang University**, Seoul, Korea • Matthew Gross, **Konkuk University**, Seoul, Korea • Matthew Stivener, **Santa Monica College**, California, USA • Pawadee Srisang, **Burapha University**, Chantaburi, Thailand • Steven M. Rashba, **University of Bridgeport**, Connecticut, USA • Sudatip Prapunta, **Prince of Songkla University**, Trang, Thailand • Tony Carnerie, **University of California San Diego**, California, USA

Photo Credits

Text Credit

Table of Contents

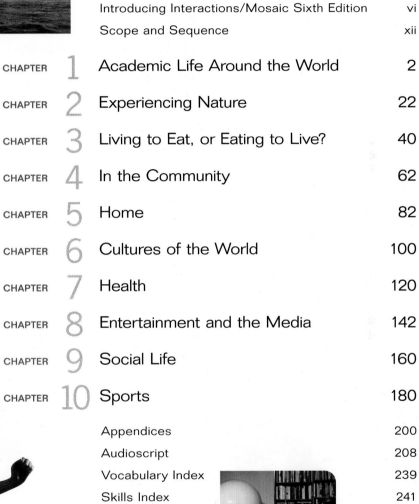

A 21st-Century Course for the Modern Student

Interactions/Mosaic prepares students for university classes by fully integrating every aspect of student life. Based on 28 years of classroom-tested best practices, the new and revised content, fresh modern look, and new online component make this the perfect series for contemporary classrooms.

Proven Instruction that Ensures Academic Success

Modern Content:
From social networking to gender issues and from academic honesty to discussions of Skype, *Interactions/ Mosaic* keeps students connected to learning by selecting topics that are interesting and relevant to modern students.

Digital Component:
The fully integrated online course offers a rich environment that expands students' learning and supports teachers' teaching with automatically graded practice, assessment, classroom presentation tools, online community, and more.

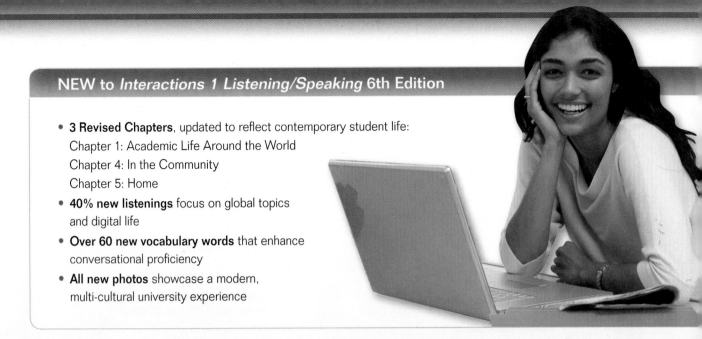

NEW to *Interactions 1 Listening/Speaking* 6th Edition

- **3 Revised Chapters**, updated to reflect contemporary student life:
  Chapter 1: Academic Life Around the World
  Chapter 4: In the Community
  Chapter 5: Home
- **40% new listenings** focus on global topics and digital life
- **Over 60 new vocabulary words** that enhance conversational proficiency
- **All new photos** showcase a modern, multi-cultural university experience

Emphasis on Vocabulary:

Each chapter teaches vocabulary intensively and comprehensively. This focus on learning new words is informed by more than 28 years of classroom testing and provides students with the exact language they need to communicate confidently and fluently.

Practical Critical Thinking:

Students develop their ability to synthesize, analyze, and apply information from different sources in a variety of contexts: from comparing academic articles to negotiating informal conversations.

Highlights of *Interactions 1 Listening/Speaking* 6th Edition

Part 1: Conversation Each chapter begins with conversations relating to contemporary academic life. The activities that follow help students develop important listening skills.

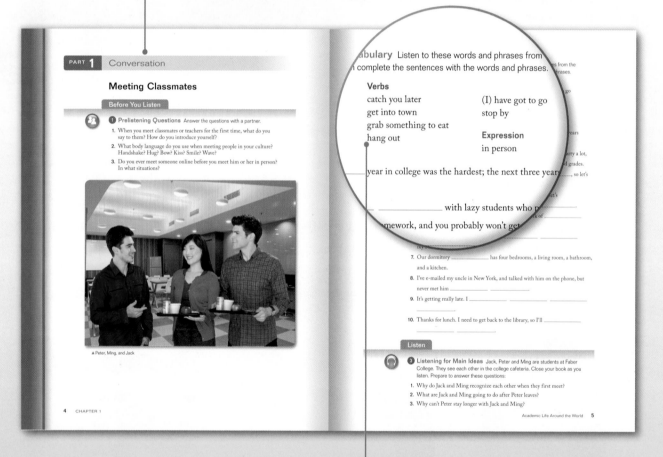

Emphasis on Vocabulary Each chapter presents, practices, and carefully recycles vocabulary-learning strategies and vocabulary words essential to the modern student.

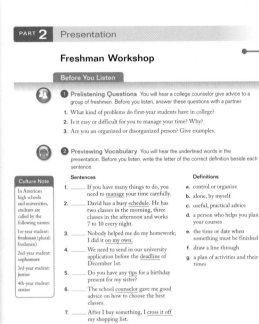

PART 2 Presentation

Freshman Workshop

Before You Listen

1 Prelistening Questions You will hear a college counselor give advice to a group of freshmen. Before you listen, answer these questions with a partner.

1. What kind of problems do first-year students have in college?
2. Is it easy or difficult for you to manage your time? Why?
3. Are you an organized or disorganized person? Give examples.

2 Previewing Vocabulary You will hear the underlined words in the presentation. Before you listen, write the letter of the correct definition beside each sentence.

Culture Note

In American high schools and universities, students are called by the following names:

1st-year student: freshman (plural: freshmen)

2nd-year student: sophomore

3rd-year student: junior

4th-year student: senior

Sentences

1. _____ If you have many things to do, you need to manage your time carefully.
2. _____ David has a busy schedule. He has two classes in the morning, three classes in the afternoon and works 7 to 10 every night.
3. _____ Nobody helped me do my homework; I did it on my own.
4. _____ We need to send in our university application before the deadline of December 1st.
5. _____ Do you have any tips for a birthday present for my sister?
6. _____ The school counselor gave me good advice on how to choose the best classes.
7. _____ After I buy something, I cross it off my shopping list.

Definitions

a. control or organize
b. alone, by myself
c. useful, practical advice
d. a person who helps you plan your courses
e. the time or date when something must be finished
f. draw a line through
g. a plan of activities and their times

12 CHAPTER 1

Part 2: Presentation
Students focus on functional language and listening to longer presentations, including academic lectures.

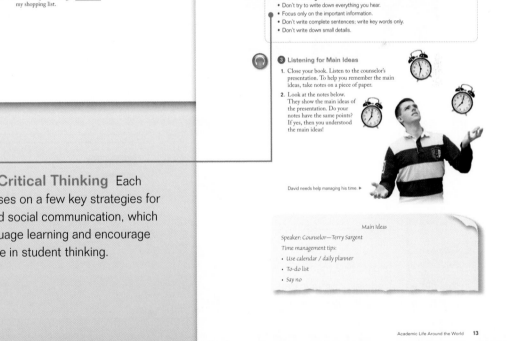

Listen

Strategy

Hints for Taking Notes
- Don't try to write down everything you hear.
- Focus only on the important information.
- Don't write complete sentences; write key words only.
- Don't write down small details.

3 Listening for Main Ideas

1. Close your book. Listen to the counselor's presentation. To help you remember the main ideas, take notes on a piece of paper.
2. Look at the notes below. They show the main ideas of the presentation. Do your notes have the same points? If yes, then you understood the main ideas!

David needs help managing his time. ►

Main Ideas

Speaker: Counselor—Terry Sargent

Time management tips:
- Use calendar / daily planner
- To-do list
- Say no

Academic Life Around the World 13

Practical Critical Thinking
Each chapter focuses on a few key strategies for academic and social communication, which support language learning and encourage independence in student thinking.

FOCUS ON TESTING

TOEFL® iBT

Using Context Clues

If you don't understand everything that English speakers say, you probably try to guess the meaning. How do you do this?

* Listen to clues, or signals, that help you guess.
* Words that you already know can be clues to new words.
* Grammar, stress, and intonation can also be clues to meaning.

Read the sentence below. Try to guess the meaning of the new word from all the other words you know.

Studying biology is a (prerequisite) to applying for medical school.

↓ clue   ↓ (new word)   ↓ clue

You probably understood that you must study biology *before* you can go to medical school, and so *prerequisite* means something it is necessary for you to complete before you start something else.

Many tests such as the TOEFL® iBT, or the IELTS measure your academic listening and speaking abilities. This activity, and others in the book, will develop your social and academic communication abilities, and help you succeed on a variety of standardized tests.

Using Context Clues

Listen to a conversation between Ming, Peter, and Peter's new roommate, Kenji.

1. The conversation is in five parts. Listen to the beginning of each part. Then listen to the question.
2. Stop the recording after the question and choose the best answer to each question.
3. In the Clues column, write the words that helped you choose your answer.
4. Start the recording again. Listen to the last part of each conversation to hear the correct answer.

▲ Ming

▲ Peter

▲ Kenji

Academic Life Around the World **15**

Part 3: Strategies for Better Listening and Speaking Impactful listening exercises help students practice getting meaning from context.

Answers	Clues
1. Ⓐ at a campus cafeteria Ⓑ at the library Ⓒ at a movie theater	*hungry, crowded, lunchtime*
2. Ⓐ computers Ⓑ textbooks Ⓒ businesses	
3. Ⓐ work hard Ⓑ study Ⓒ exercise	
4. Ⓐ The students are happy to hear from their parents. Ⓑ The parents are worried about the students. Ⓒ The students are worried about their parents.	
5. Ⓐ He is not good at time management. Ⓑ He forgot to study for the test. Ⓒ He will go to a party at Jack's all night.	

Talk It Over

FOCUS

Understanding Body Language

If you watch someone speaking, **body language**—gestures, facial expressions, and eye contact—can give you important clues to help you understand the speaker.

 1 Using Body Language With your class, discuss what you think the gestures on the next page mean.

16 CHAPTER 1

Communication for the Modern Student A focus on real-life and academic communication prepares students for success in school and in life.

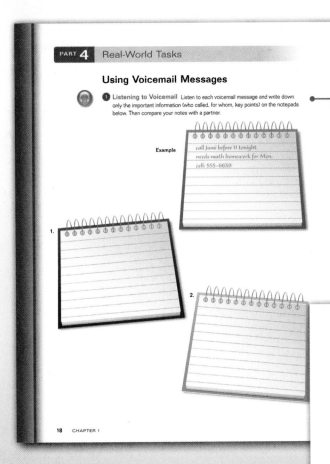

Using Voicemail Messages

1 **Listening to Voicemail** Listen to each voicemail message and write down only the important information (who called, for whom, key points) on the notepads below. Then compare your notes with a partner.

Example

call Jumi before 11 tonight
needs math homework for Mon.
cell: 555-6639

1.

2.

18 CHAPTER 1

Part 4: Real-World Tasks Students learn to apply their listening and speaking skills to a variety of practical interactions such as using voicemail.

Self-Assessment Log

Check (✓) the words you learned in this chapter.

Nouns	Verbs	Expressions
anybody else	catch you later	in person
counselor	cross it off	on your own
deadline	get into town	
freshman (freshm		
schedule	stop by	
suit		

eck (✓) the things you did in this chapter. How

Very well

I can listen to and practice stress
and reductions.   ☐

I can listen to and pronounce -s endings.   ☐

I can introduce myself and others.   ☐

I can take notes about the main ideas
and specific details of a presentation.   ☐

I can summarize my notes.   ☐

I can guess meanings from context.   ☐

I can understand and talk about body
guage.   ☐

isten to and summarize key points
I liked   ail message.

Results for Students A carefully structured program presents and practices academic skills and strategies purposefully, leading to strong student results and more independent learners.

Scope and Sequence

Chapter	Listening	Speaking
1 Academic Life Around the World p2 	Listening for main ideas and details Distinguishing among –s endings Listening to a counselor's presentation Listening to voicemail messages	Introducing yourself and others Discussing body language Summarizing voicemail messages Calling for specific information
2 Experiencing Nature p22 	Listening for main ideas and details Distinguishing between *can* and *can't* Listening to a story about camping Listening to weather forecasts	Discussing vacation plans Talking about abilities Talking about the weather and seasons Expressing likes and dislikes
3 Living to Eat, or Eating to Live? p40 	Listening for main ideas and details Distinguishing between *teens* and *tens* Listening to radio advice on healthy eating Connecting native foods to their locations	Interviewing people about food shopping Using count and non-count nouns in questions Comparing eating habits at home and when traveling Ordering food Refusing food politely
4 In the Community p62 	Listening for main ideas and details Following directions on a map Listening to a student talk about her college experience	Talking about community activities such as volunteering Describing locations in a city Comparing colleges in small towns and cities Asking for and giving directions

Critical-Thinking Skills	Vocabulary Building	Pronunciation	Focus on Testing
Guessing meaning from context Distinguishing between main ideas and details Summarizing main ideas Interpreting body language	Expressions used in introductions Terms related to arrival at college or at a university Casual expressions for making new friends Terms used in summarizing voice mails	Identifying and practicing stressed words Comparing reduced and unreduced pronunciation Pronouncing –s endings	**TOEFL iBT** Using context clues to guess the correct answers to questions
Interpreting a photo Using a T-chart to compare two sides of a topic Distinguishing main ideas from details Summarizing ideas using keywords	Terms to express abilities Terms to describe the weather and seasons Terms to talk about likes and dislikes	Identifying and practicing stressed words Comparing reduced and unreduced pronunciation Pronouncing *can* and *can't*	**TOEFL iBT** Using context clues to identify seasons
Interpreting a photo Interviewing with possible follow-up questions Taking notes on causes and effects Explaining a process Speculating on the outcome of a situation	Terms used in shopping for food at a market Terms to talk about healthy eating Count and non-count nouns to express quantities of food Terms for ordering food in a restaurant Polite refusals	Identifying and practicing stressed words Comparing reduced and unreduced pronunciation Pronouncing *teens* and *tens*	**TOEFL iBT** Using context clues to guess restaurant types
Interpreting a photo Using a concept map to make comparisons Summarizing ideas using keywords	Terms to describe locations in the city Expressions for giving and asking for directions	Identifying and practicing stressed words Comparing reduced and unreduced pronunciation	**TOEFL iBT** Using context clues to guess locations

Scope and Sequence

Chapter	Listening	Speaking
5 Home p82 	Listening for main ideas and details Listening to conversations about renting an apartment and student housing Following home-exchange instructions Following instructions on where to put furniture	Talking about finding somewhere to live Asking for information about housing ads Making and answering requests for apartment repairs
6 Cultures of the World p100 	Listening for main ideas and details Listening to a lecture about coming-of-age ceremonies Listening to instructions for setting a formal dinner table	Comparing customs Discussing minimum age requirements in different cultures Talking about dining customs and table manners Apologizing
7 Health p120 	Listening for main ideas and details Listening to a health club tour Distinguishing between rising and falling intonation in tag questions Listening to medical advice Listening to phone messages from healthcare professionals	Forming and using tag questions with correct intonation Asking for and giving advice Discussing smoking—advertising and laws Talking to healthcare workers: making appointments by phone
8 Entertainment and the Media p142 	Listening for main ideas and details Listening to opinions about television Listening to a news report Listening to radio ads	Expressing, agreeing with, and disagreeing with opinions Discussing the qualities of good ads Talking about types of TV programs Describing favorite TV shows and movies

Critical-Thinking Skills	Vocabulary Building	Pronunciation	Focus on Testing
Interpreting a photo and an ad Taking notes that separate advantages from disadvantages Using a multi-column chart to fill in notes to organize information Summarizing ideas using keywords	Terms to talk about apartments and student housing Common verbs related to moving Expressions for making and answering requests for information Verbs and frequent expressions used to explain home maintenance	Identifying and practicing stressed words Comparing reduced and unreduced pronunciation Pronouncing past tense –ed endings	**TOEFL iBT** Using context clues to guess what speakers are implying
Interpreting a photo Using a matrix diagram to organize ideas Summarizing ideas using keywords	Adjectives describing feelings Expressions for apologizing Correct use of 'I'm sorry' vs. 'Excuse me' Terms used related to table settings and table manners	Identifying and practicing stressed words Comparing reduced and unreduced pronunciation	**TOEFL iBT** Using context clues to identify culturally incorrect behaviors
Interpreting a photo Using a problem-solution chart to list and clarify symptoms and treatments Completing a questionnaire on stress and interpreting the score Summarizing a medical visit using keywords	Terms connected with a health club Terms describing symptoms and remedies Expressions for giving and accepting advice Terms used in expressing agreement or disagreement	Identifying and practicing stressed words Contrasting rising and falling intonation in tag questions	**TOEFL iBT** Using context clues to identify unusual details within situations
Interpreting a photo Identifying the four "W's" in a news report Summarizing news reports using keywords Locating information in a TV guide.	Terms for expressing opinions, agreeing and disagreeing Terms related to TV-watching habits Terms to describe types of TV programs	Identifying and practicing stressed words Comparing reduced and unreduced pronunciation	**TOEFL iBT** Using context clues to identify products and services in commercials

Scope and Sequence

Chapter	Listening	Speaking
9 Social Life p160 	Listening for main ideas and details Interpreting intonation used with exclamations Listening to a conversation on dating and a marriage match Listening to phone calls on entertainment	Discussing dating customs Giving and accepting compliments Discussing parties Discussing preferences and experiences in spending free time
10 Sports p180 	Listening for main ideas and details Listening to a conversation about martial arts Listening to a talk by a female wrestler Listening to a sportscast	Explaining a sport Giving and understanding instructions Playing "Twenty Questions" Using correct nouns and verbs to describe sports and athletes

Critical-Thinking Skills	Vocabulary Building	Pronunciation	Focus on Testing
Interpreting a photo Comparing alternatives—selecting the best match Gathering information from entertainment advertisements Summarizing research on upcoming events	Terms connected with friendship and dating Exclamations Expressions used in giving and accepting compliments Terms to talk about personal qualities and compatibility Terms connected with parties and common entertainment activities	Identifying and practicing stressed words Using appropriate intonation with exclamations	**TOEFL® iBT** Using context clues to guess the nature of interpersonal relationships
Interpreting a photo Organizing notes into an outline Summarizing a speech using key words	Nouns vs. verbs to describe sports and athletes Terms used in a sportscast Terms for giving instructions Terms to ensure comprehension Terms to ask for clarification	Identifying and practicing stressed words Comparing reduced and unreduced pronunciation Pronouncing the North American *t* Dropping the *h* sound in unstressed words	**TOEFL® iBT** Using context clues to identify different sports

Introducing the Interactions 1
Listening/Speaking Characters

Name: Ali
Nationality: American

Name: Nancy
Nationality: American

Name: Kenji
Nationality: Japanese

Name: Salma
Nationality: Lebanese

Name: Ming
Nationality: Chinese

Name: Lee
Nationality: Korean

Name: Peter
Nationality: Puerto Rican

Name: Yolanda
Nationality: American

Name: Jack
Nationality: American

Name: Andrew
Nationality: American

1 Academic Life Around the World

> "If you think education is expensive, try ignorance."
>
> Derek Curtis Bok,
> former president of Harvard University

In this
CHAPTER

Conversation Meeting Classmates

Presentation Freshman Workshop

Getting Meaning from Context
Using Verbal and Non-Verbal Clues

Real-World Tasks Using Voicemail Messages

Connecting to the Topic

1 Look at the people in the photo. Who are they, and what do you think their relationship is to each other?

2 How do you prefer to communicate with your school friends: by texting, phone, or Facebook? Why?

3 What are some of the pressures high school and university students are facing today? What can students do to reduce stress?

Meeting Classmates

Before You Listen

1 Prelistening Questions Answer the questions with a partner.

1. When you meet classmates or teachers for the first time, what do you say to them? How do you introduce yourself?

2. What body language do you use when meeting people in your culture? Handshake? Hug? Bow? Kiss? Smile? Wave?

3. Do you ever meet someone online before you meet him or her in person? In what situations?

▲ Peter, Ming, and Jack

2 Previewing Vocabulary Listen to these words and phrases from the conversation. Then complete the sentences with the words and phrases.

Nouns	Verbs	
anybody else	catch you later	(I) have got to go (gotta go)
freshman	get into town	stop by
suite	grab something to eat	
	hang out	**Expression**
		in person

1. My _____ year in college was the hardest; the next three years got easier.

2. If you _____ _____ with lazy students who party a lot, you'll never finish your homework, and you probably won't get good grades.

3. My brother just _____ _____ _____, so let's pick him up at the airport.

4. Are you hungry? Chicken Delish is right across the street—let's

   _____ _____ _____ _____.

5. We have an extra ticket for the game, but I can't think of _____

   _____ to invite.

6. If you're ever in my dormitory, please _____ _____

   my room for a cup of tea.

7. Our dormitory _____ has four bedrooms, a living room, a bathroom, and a kitchen.

8. I've e-mailed my uncle in New York, and talked with him on the phone, but never met him _____ _____.

9. It's getting really late. I _____ _____ _____

   _____.

10. Thanks for lunch. I need to get back to the library, so I'll _____

    _____ _____.

Listen

3 Listening for Main Ideas Jack, Peter and Ming are students at Faber College. They see each other in the college cafeteria. Close your book as you listen. Prepare to answer these questions:

1. Why do Jack and Ming recognize each other when they first meet?
2. What are Jack and Ming going to do after Peter leaves?
3. Why can't Peter stay longer with Jack and Ming?

Academic Life Around the World **5**

4 **Listening for Details** Listen to the conversation again if necessary. Write *T* if a statement is true and *F* if it is false.

1. _____ Ming's parents are from San Francisco.

2. _____ Jack lives in the building where he, Ming and Peter are all talking.

3. _____ Ming enjoyed meeting Peter.

Stress

F⦿CUS

In spoken English, important words are stressed. This means that they are spoken louder, longer, or higher than other words. Stressed words usually give the most important information. These kinds of words are usually stressed: verbs, nouns, adjectives, adverbs, numbers, and negatives like *isn't*, *don't*, and *can't*.

Example

My **name** is **Peter.**

I'm in **suite two-ten.**

Maybe you can **stop by.**

Ming and **Jack** are the **same age.**

5 **Listening for Stressed Words** Listen to the conversation again. Some of the stressed words are missing. During each pause, repeat the phrase or sentence. Then fill in the blanks with the words you hear.

Jack, Ming and Peter are students at Faber College. They see each other in the college cafeteria.

Jack: _____ me—Aren't you Ming? Ming Lee?

Ming: Uh... _____—oh _____—you're

_____! Great to _____ you in person.

Jack: You _____ a little _____ online.

Ming: You _____; you're _____.

Jack: Well, I was _____ _____ when we video

chatted. So, um, have you met _____ _____?

I mean from the freshman _____ group?

Ming: A _____ guys—not many. When did you get into

_____?

Jack: I got here _____—still got boxes _____...

Oh, and Ming, this is _____. Peter, Ming.

Peter: Nice to meet you. Ming…

Ming: Nice to meet you.

Peter: Are you from…

Ming: … from San Francisco—my _____ are from _____ _____, though.

Peter: Cool. I plan to spend my _____ _____ in Hong Kong. Excuse me. Oh that's my new _____ texting. He _____ a _____ to the room. Sorry, I've got to go.

Jack: Wanna eat _____ with us first?

Peter: Nah, I can _____ something later. Jack, where did you say you _____?

Jack: _____ in suite 33. _____ _____ sometime.

Peter: I will. Hope to _____ you, _____, Ming.

Ming: Yeah, _____ me on Facebook. Ming Lee—L-E-E.

Peter: Okay. I will. Let's _____ _____ sometime…. Anyway, see you _____ later. Have a nice dinner.

Jack: Thanks. Catch you later.

Now read the conversation with two other classmates. Practice stressing words correctly.

Reductions

FOCUS

In spoken English, important words are usually stressed. Other words are not stressed; they are often *reduced* or *shortened*. These kinds of words are often reduced: prepositions, articles, pronouns, forms of the verb *to be,* and the words *and, or,* and *but.*

Unreduced Pronunciation	Reduced Pronunciation*
Do you want to…	D'ya* wanna…
I've got to go.	I've gotta* go.
Great to meet you.	Greata meetcha*.

Reduced pronunciation is a natural part of spoken English. Recognizing reduced forms of words will help you understand both formal and informal speech.

*Note: The reduced forms are not acceptable spellings in written English.

6 **Comparing Unreduced and Reduced Pronunciation** The following sentences come from the conversation. Listen for the difference between unreduced and reduced pronunciation. Repeat both forms after the speaker.

Unreduced Pronunciation	Reduced Pronunciation
1. Aren't you Ming?	Arncha Ming?
2. Nice to meet you.	Niceta meetcha.
3. Do you want to eat with us first?	D'ya wanna eat with us first?
4. Sorry. I have got to go.	Sorry, I've gotta go.
5. When did you get into town?	Whendja get into town?

7 **Listening for Reductions** Listen to the following sentences. You'll hear the reduced pronunciations of some words. Repeat each sentence during the pause. Then write the unreduced forms of the missing words in the blanks.

1. What _____ _____ do last weekend?

2. We've _____ _____ study tonight.

3. Jack, _____ _____ _____ _____

   eat at the cafeteria?

4. I can _____ _____ in half an hour.

5. _____ _____ finished with the test yet?

With a partner, read the sentences. Practice using reduced pronunciation.

After You Listen

8 **Reviewing Vocabulary** Work in pairs: Student A should look at page 200. Student B should look at page 204.

Pronunciation

FOCUS

The -s Ending

The -s at the end of words can be pronounced in three different ways. The pronunciation depends on the last sound of the word:

/iz/ after -ch, -sh, -s, -x, and -z endings.

> **Examples** teaches, boxes, passes, brushes

/s/ after voiceless -k, -f, -p, or -t endings.

> **Examples** walks, stops, hits, puts

/z/ after voiced endings.

> **Examples** carries, brings, father's, rides

9 Distinguishing Among -s Endings Listen and write the words. Then check the sound you hear. The first one is done as an example.

		/iz/	/s/	/z/
1.	_plays_	☐	☐	☑
2.	_____	☐	☐	☐
3.	_____	☐	☐	☐
4.	_____	☐	☐	☐
5.	_____	☐	☐	☐
6.	_____	☐	☐	☐
7.	_____	☐	☐	☐
8.	_____	☐	☐	☐
9.	_____	☐	☐	☐
10.	_____	☐	☐	☐

10 Pronouncing -s Endings Work with a partner. Ask and answer the following questions in complete sentences. Pay attention to the pronunciation of the -s endings.

1. Where does your teacher work?
2. What does he or she teach?
3. How much homework does your teacher give you?
4. When does your class begin?
5. When does it end?
6. What technology tools does your teacher use in class?
7. How long does it take for you to get to school?
8. What kind of electronic devices are popular with your classmates?
9. Have you ever taken online courses?
10. What does a student do if he or she wants to ask a question in class?

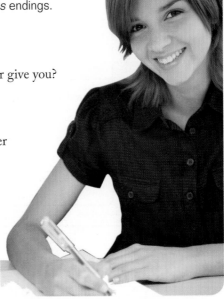

▲ "My teacher works at three different colleges. She also writes textbooks."

FOCUS

Introducing Yourself and Others

Read this part of the conversation carefully, and notice how Jack introduces Ming and Peter informally.

Jack: ... Ming, this is Peter... Peter, Ming.

Peter: Nice to meet you. Ming...

Ming: Nice to meet you.

The following expressions are often used to introduce yourself or others.

<table>
<tr><td colspan="2">Functions</td><td colspan="3">Expressions</td></tr>
<tr><td></td><td></td><td>Speaker A</td><td>Speaker B</td><td>Speaker C</td></tr>
<tr><td rowspan="3">Introducing Others</td><td></td><td>Abdul, this is my friend, Steve.</td><td>Hi, Steve.</td><td>Nice to meet you.</td></tr>
<tr><td></td><td>Linda, I'd like you to meet my roommate, Eunnim.</td><td>Good to meet you, Eunnim.</td><td>You, too.</td></tr>
<tr><td></td><td>Mom, I'd like to introduce you to Mr. Ogawa. He is my English teacher.</td><td>Pleasure to meet you.</td><td>Same here.</td></tr>
<tr><td rowspan="2">Introducing Yourself</td><td></td><td>Hi, I'm Caroline. I'm your neighbor, in Apartment 810.</td><td>Nice to meet you.</td><td></td></tr>
<tr><td></td><td>Hello. My name is Ellen. I work in the office next door.</td><td>Hi, Ellen. I'm Ricardo.</td><td></td></tr>
</table>

> **Culture Note**
>
> When English speakers introduce someone, they usually add some information about the person, such as the person's type of work, their home country, or an interesting fact about them.

11 **Making Introductions** Practice introducing classmates to each other.

1. Sit in a circle if possible.

2. Write your first name on a card and place it where everyone can see it.

3. Ask the student next to you three or four questions such as the following:

- Where are you from? Where do you live now?
- What do you do? Are you a full-time student, or do you work and go to school part-time?
- What do you enjoy doing in your free time?

4. Introduce your partner to several other students. Try to use different expressions from the chart on page 10.

Example

Berto, this is Jin. Jin, this is Berto. Berto is from Mexico. He's a business student. And he is a big soccer fan.

5. Put away your name cards. Walk around the room to check whose names you can remember, or whose names you forgot. Use expressions like these:

- You're Chen, right?
- Sorry—what was your name again?
- Excuse me, I didn't catch your name.
- I'm sorry, could you tell me your name again?

▲ ""I'm sorry, what was your name again?"

12 Role-Play: A First Meeting David and Mary are new students at the same school. They meet for the first time on a street near campus where they accidentally bump into each other. Mary doesn't realize that David is one of her many Facebook friends. What do they say to each other? Will they meet again? Prepare a funny conversation with a partner. Then try to remember the conversation and put on the "skit" for the class.

▲ David and Mary

Freshman Workshop

Before You Listen

1 **Prelistening Questions** You will hear a college counselor give advice to a group of freshmen. Before you listen, answer these questions with a partner.

1. What kind of problems do first-year students have in college?
2. Is it easy or difficult for you to manage your time? Why?
3. Are you an organized or disorganized person? Give examples.

2 **Previewing Vocabulary** You will hear the underlined words in the presentation. Before you listen, write the letter of the correct definition beside each sentence.

Culture Note

In American high schools and universities, students are called by the following names:

1st-year student: **freshman** (plural: freshmen)

2nd-year student: **sophomore**

3rd-year student: **junior**

4th-year student: **senior**

Sentences

1. _____ If you have many things to do, you need to manage your time carefully.

2. _____ David has a busy schedule. He has two classes in the morning, three classes in the afternoon and works 7 to 10 every night.

3. _____ Nobody helped me do my homework; I did it on my own.

4. _____ We need to send in our university application before the deadline of December 1st.

5. _____ Do you have any tips for a birthday present for my sister?

6. _____ The school counselor gave me good advice on how to choose the best classes.

7. _____ After I buy something, I cross it off my shopping list.

Definitions

a. control or organize

b. alone, by myself

c. useful, practical advice

d. a person who helps you plan your courses

e. the time or date when something must be finished

f. draw a line through

g. a plan of activities and their times

Strategy

Hints for Taking Notes
- Don't try to write down everything you hear.
- Focus only on the important information.
- Don't write complete sentences; write key words only.
- Don't write down small details.

3 Listening for Main Ideas

1. Close your book. Listen to the counselor's presentation. To help you remember the main ideas, take notes on a piece of paper.

2. Look at the notes below. They show the main ideas of the presentation. Do your notes have the same points? If yes, then you understood the main ideas!

David needs help managing his time. ▶

Main Ideas

Speaker: Counselor—Terry Sargent

Time management tips:

• Use calendar / daily planner

• To-do list

• Say no

4 **Listening for Specific Information** Listen to the presentation again. This time, add details to the main ideas.

Main Ideas and Details

Speaker: Counselor—Terry Sargent

Time management tips:

• Use calendar / daily planner

_____

• To-do list

_____

• Say no

_____

After You Listen

5 **Summarizing Main Ideas** Compare notes with a partner. Summarize the presentation in your own words. As you speak, look at your notes to help you remember.

Example

"In this speech, a counselor speaks to new students. She gives tips on..."

6 **Reviewing Vocabulary** Ask and answer the following questions with a partner. Use the underlined vocabulary in your answers.

1. What helps you to manage your schedule? Do you use a calendar, a to-do list or anything else?
2. Before a test, do you prefer to study on your own or with a group of students? Why?
3. What tips can you give a student who always does her homework at the last minute?
4. What kind of personality is necessary to be a good counselor?
5. What kind of deadlines do you have in the next four weeks (pay bills, finish a school project, etc.)?

FOCUS ON TESTING

TOEFL® iBT

Using Context Clues

If you don't understand everything that English speakers say, you probably try to guess the meaning. How do you do this?

- Listen to clues, or signals, that help you guess.
- Words that you already know can be clues to new words.
- Grammar, stress, and intonation can also be clues to meaning.

Read the sentence below. Try to guess the meaning of the new word from all the other words you know.

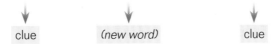

Studying biology is a (*prerequisite*) to *applying for medical school.*

| | | |
| clue | (new word) | clue |

You probably understood that you must study biology *before* you can go to medical school, and so *prerequisite* means something it is necessary for you to complete before you start something else.

Many tests such as the TOEFL® iBT, or the IELTS measure your academic listening and speaking abilities. This activity, and others in the book, will develop your social and academic communication abilities, and help you succeed on a variety of standardized tests.

Using Context Clues

Listen to a conversation between Ming, Peter, and Peter's new roommate, Kenji.

1. The conversation is in five parts. Listen to the beginning of each part. Then listen to the question.
2. Stop the recording after the question and choose the best answer to each question.
3. In the Clues column, write the words that helped you choose your answer.
4. Start the recording again. Listen to the last part of each conversation to hear the correct answer.

▲ Ming

▲ Peter

▲ Kenji

TOEFL® is a registered trademark of Educational Testing Service (ETS). This product is not endorsed or approved by ETS.

Answers	Clues
1. (A) at a campus cafeteria (B) at the library (C) at a movie theater	*hungry, crowded, lunchtime*
2. (A) computers (B) textbooks (C) businesses	
3. (A) work hard (B) study (C) exercise	
4. (A) The students are happy to hear from their parents. (B) The parents are worried about the students. (C) The students are worried about their parents.	
5. (A) He is not good at time management. (B) He forgot to study for the test. (C) He will go to a party at Jack's all night.	

Talk It Over

FOCUS

Understanding Body Language

If you watch someone speaking, **body language**—gestures, facial expressions, and eye contact—can give you important clues to help you understand the speaker.

1 Using Body Language With your class, discuss what you think the gestures on the next page mean.

Use body language to show the following situations.

1. You don't know the answer to the question.
2. You think that the class is boring.
3. You can't hear what someone is saying.
4. Someone on the phone is talking too much.
5. You like something.

Using Voicemail Messages

1 **Listening to Voicemail**   Listen to each voicemail message and write down only the important information (who called, for whom, key points) on the notepads below. Then compare your notes with a partner.

Example

call Jumi before 11 tonight
needs math homework for Mon.
cell: 555–6639

1.

2.

3.

4.

5.

6.

2 **Summarizing Phone Messages** Work with a partner. Using your notes from the six messages, take turns reporting and summarizing the important information you remember from each message. Practice asking each other good follow-up questions.

Example

A: Jumi wants Kenji to call her tonight before 11.

B: Oh. Why did she call?

A: She wants the homework from their math class for Monday.

B: Uh huh—why does she need it?

A: She's still sick.

B: Does Kenji have her number?

A: He might—but she left her cell number—it's 555-6639

B: Great.

Strategy

Telephone Numbers

When saying telephone numbers, English speakers will understand you better if you:

- pause after the area code
- pause after the first three numbers, and between the next two pairs of numbers
- raise your voice before every pause
- lower your voice at the end

Example

area code 310 555 0162

three-one-zero   five-five-five   zero-one   six-two

3 Calling for Information Ming calls Faber College about parking and talks to an administrative assistant. Listen to her conversation and complete the parking assistant's application notes:

PARKING PERMIT APPLICATION

Parking Lot requested: _____

Permit Holder: Name: (last) _____ (first) _____

Student I.D.: _____

Vehicle: Year _____ Make: _____ Model: _____

License Plate: Number _____ State: _____

Permit issued for: Semester _____ (or) Year _____

Amount Due: $_____

4 Role-Play Compare your application notes with a partner. Then role-play Ming and the parking assistant from your notes. Pronounce numbers carefully!

Self-Assessment Log

Check (✓) the words you learned in this chapter.

Nouns
- anybody else
- counselor
- deadline
- freshman (freshmen)
- schedule
- suite
- tips

Verbs
- catch you later
- cross it off
- get into town
- grab something to eat
- hang out
- (I) have got to go (gotta go)
- manage
- stop by

Expressions
- in person
- on your own

Check (✓) the things you did in this chapter. How well can you do each one?

	Very well	Fairly well	Not very well
I can listen to and practice stress and reductions.	☐	☐	☐
I can listen to and pronounce -s endings.	☐	☐	☐
I can introduce myself and others.	☐	☐	☐
I can take notes about the main ideas and specific details of a presentation.	☐	☐	☐
I can summarize my notes.	☐	☐	☐
I can guess meanings from context.	☐	☐	☐
I can understand and talk about body language.	☐	☐	☐
I can listen to and summarize key points of a voicemail message.	☐	☐	☐

Write about what you did in this chapter.

In this chapter,

I learned _____

_____

I liked _____

_____

2 Experiencing Nature

"In every walk with nature, one receives far more than he seeks.

John Muir
American naturalist

Connecting to the Topic

1. Look at the photo. What do you see? Would you like to be in this place? Why or why not?

2. What kinds of outdoor activities do you enjoy?

3. What is your favorite season? Why?

Vacation Plans

Before You Listen

1 **Prelistening Questions** Look at the photo. Answer the questions with a partner.

1. What are Ming, Peter, and Jack thinking about?
2. Describe your perfect outdoor vacation. Where would you go? What would you do there?

▼ Ming, Peter, and Jack

2 Previewing Vocabulary Listen to these words and phrases from the conversation. Complete the sentences with these words and phrases.

Nouns	Verb	Adjectives	Expressions
chance of	get a tan	extra	How come…?
degrees		freezing	it's pouring (rain)
weather		sick of	
forecast		(verb + *-ing*)	

1. **A:** Wow. _____ you're all wet?

   B: Because _____ outside, and I forgot my umbrella.

2. In the summer, I love to lie in the sun and _____.

3. The weather report in the newspaper says there's a 90 percent

   _____ snow tomorrow. Be sure to dress warm.

4. It's 20 _____ Celsius* outside. You don't need a sweater.

5. When are we going to get to Las Vegas? We've been on the road for six hours.

   I am _____ driving.

6. **A:** Did you hear the _____

   _____ for tomorrow on
   the news?

   B: Yes. It's going to be sunny and warm.
   A perfect day for the beach!

7. **A:** Why don't you turn on the heater?

   It's _____ in this room!

   B: It's broken. We'll have to sleep in our coats
   tonight.

8. Do you have an _____

   jacket? I forgot mine at home.

   *Equal to about 68° Fahrenheit.

▲ It's pouring rain.

Listen

3 Listening for Main Ideas Jack, Peter, and Ming are talking about weather and vacations. Close your book as you listen. Prepare to answer these questions.

1. Why does Peter want to go on vacation soon?

2. Where does Ming prefer to go on vacation?

3. What do Jack and Peter agree about?

Compare and discuss your answers with a partner.

4 **Listening for Details** Listen again if necessary. Write *T* if a statement is true and *F* if it is false.

1. _____ It is almost the end of the school year.

2. _____ Jack has never tried skiing.

3. _____ The weather isn't going to be better tomorrow.

Stress

5 **Listening for Stressed Words** Listen to the conversation again. Some of the stressed words are missing. During each pause, repeat the phrase or sentence. Then fill in the blanks with words you hear.

Culture Note

In North America, the school year begins in September, and there is a long vacation in December called **winter break.** In most cases, school starts again after the New Year.

Peter: Wow. Look. It's pouring _____! I

_____ this weather. When does winter

_____ start?

Jack: Winter break? It's only _____.

Peter: I know, but I'm _____ of studying. I want to go someplace

_____ and lie on the _____ for a week.

Someplace where it's _____ and dry. Florida or Hawaii,

maybe?

Jack: Yeah. Where we can go _____ and snorkeling and get a

great _____. Now _____ my idea of a

perfect vacation.

Ming: Not mine. I can't swim very well, and I _____ like lying in

the _____.

Peter: Oh, yeah? How come?

Ming: I don't know. I just prefer the _____, especially in winter.

I _____ snowboarding. In fact, I'm _____

to go to Bear Mountain with some friends in _____. Do

you guys want to _____?

Jack: No thanks. I went there _____ year. I was

_____ the whole time. Anyway, I don't know how to

_____ very well. Last year I _____ about

a hundred times.

Ming: Peter, how about you?

Peter: Sorry, I'm like Jack. I don't want to go ＿＿＿＿＿＿ where it's below 70 ＿＿＿＿＿＿.

Jack: By the way, what's the ＿＿＿＿＿＿ forecast for tomorrow?

Ming: The ＿＿＿＿＿＿ as today. ＿＿＿＿＿＿, cold, and a 90 percent ＿＿＿＿＿＿ of rain.

Jack: Oh, no! I ＿＿＿＿＿＿ my umbrella at the ＿＿＿＿＿＿.

Ming: You can ＿＿＿＿＿＿ mine. I've got an ＿＿＿＿＿＿ one.

Now read the conversation with two other classmates. Practice stressing words correctly.

Reductions

6 Comparing Unreduced and Reduced Pronunciation The following sentences come from the conversation. Listen for the difference between unreduced and reduced pronunciation. Repeat both forms after the speaker.

Unreduced Pronunciation	Reduced Pronunciation*
1. I am sick of this weather.	I'm sicka this weather.
2. I want to go someplace warm.	I wanna go someplace warm.
3. We can swim.	We kin swim.
4. I'm going to go to Bear Mountain.	I'm gonna go ta Bear Mountain.
5. How about you?	How bouchu?
6. I don't want to go.	I donwanna go.

  * Note: The underlined forms are not acceptable spellings in written English.

7 Listening for Reductions Listen to the following conversation. You'll hear the reduced pronunciations of some words. Repeat each sentence during the pause. Then write the unreduced forms of the missing words in the blanks.

Jack: Hi, Ming. Hi, Peter.

Ming and Peter: Hey, Jack.

Ming: What's happening?

Jack: I'm going to the campus recreation center. ＿＿＿＿＿＿ ＿＿＿＿＿＿ ＿＿＿＿＿＿ ＿＿＿＿＿＿ come?

Ming: What are you ＿＿＿＿＿＿ ＿＿＿＿＿＿ do there?

Jack: Well, it's a nice day. We ＿＿＿＿＿＿ swim ＿＿＿＿＿＿ lie in the sun.

Ming: Thanks, but I _____ _____ _____ go.

I'm too tired.

Jack: How _____ _____, Peter?

Peter: I can't. I've _____ _____ stay at home

_____ study. Maybe tomorrow.

With a partner, repeat the dialogue. Practice reduced pronunciation.

After You Listen

8 Using Vocabulary Discuss the following questions with a partner. Use the underlined vocabulary in your answers.

1. When you are <u>sick of</u> studying, what do you do to relax?
2. In your hometown, what is the coldest temperature, and what is the hottest temperature? (Use the word <u>degrees</u> in your answer.)
3. What is a safe way to <u>get a tan</u>?
4. Are you afraid to drive if <u>it's pouring rain</u>? How much <u>extra</u> time do you give yourself when you drive in bad weather?
5. What is the <u>chance of</u> rain tomorrow in the area where you live?
6. What's the best place to get the <u>weather forecast</u>: TV, newspaper, or Internet?
7. Which is worse for you: to be <u>freezing</u> or to be too hot?

Pronunciation

FOCUS

Can or *Can't*

Notice the difference between the pronunciations of *can* and *can't* in the following sentences.

I *can* méet you tomorrow.　　　I *can't* méet you tomorrow.

Can is unstressed, so the vowel is reduced. It sounds like "kin." Stress only the main verb:

can méet

Can't is stressed, so the vowel is not reduced. Stress both *can't* and the main verb:

can't méet

9 Distinguishing Between *Can* **and** *Can't* Listen and repeat each statement. Circle *Can* if the statement is affirmative and *Can't* if the statement is negative.

1. Can   Can't   6. Can   Can't
2. Can   Can't   7. Can   Can't
3. Can   Can't   8. Can   Can't
4. Can   Can't   9. Can   Can't
5. Can   Can't   10. Can   Can't

Using Language Functions

FOCUS

Talking About Abilities

You can use *can* and *can't* to talk about abilities.

Example Ming can ski, but she can't swim.

Here are some other expressions for talking about what you can and can't do:

- I'm (not) able to (+ verb)
- I (don't) know how to (+ verb)
- I wish I could (+ verb)
- I'm (not) good at (+ verb + *-ing*)
- I'm (not) really good at (+ verb + *-ing*)

Strategy

Graphic Organizer: T-Chart

T-charts can help you organize and compare two different sides of a topic.
For example:

- You can compare the advantages and disadvantages of an idea to help you make a decision to do a specific action.
- You can compare facts and opinions.
- You can list the strengths and weaknesses of an idea or of something you read or listen to.

Advantages/Disadvantages T-Chart
Topic: _____

Advantages	Disadvantages

10 Talking About Abilities Complete this chart. Then tell a partner about your abilities. Use *can, can't,* and the expressions from the list on page 29.

Topic: Abilities	
Things I Am Good At	**Things I Am Not Good At**
1.	1.
2.	2.
3.	3.
4.	4.

Example

I am good at writing essays.   I'm not good at skiing.

PART 2 Story

Camping

Before You Listen

 1 Prelistening Questions You will hear a story about camping. Before you listen, answer these questions with a partner.

1. Have you ever gone camping? Talk about this experience with your partner. Where did you go? When? With whom?
2. Why do many people enjoy camping?
3. What unpleasant or dangerous things can happen while on a camping trip?

 2 Previewing Vocabulary Listen to the underlined words and phrases. You will hear the underlined words and phrases in a story. Write the letter of the correct definition beside each sentence.

Sentences

1. _____ The view at the top of the mountain was <u>incredible</u>. The sunset was orange and purple.

2. _____ Please clean your <u>muddy</u> shoes before you come inside the house.

3. _____ When I'm sick of being in the city, I go <u>hiking</u> in the mountains.

4. _____ After the rain stopped, the sky was <u>clear</u> and sunny.

5. _____ After six months in another country, I <u>couldn't wait</u> to see my family again.

6. _____ Don't be <u>scared</u> of the dog; she is very sweet and gentle.

Definitions

a. afraid

b. walking out in nature

c. wanted to do something very much

d. unbelievable; very surprising

e. covered with wet dirt

f. not cloudy

3 **Listening for Main Ideas** A man and a woman are checking into a motel. They tell the manager a very unusual story. As you listen, answer these questions.

1. What starts all of the trouble?

2. What happens to the couple's clothes?

4 **Taking Notes on Specific Information** Listen to the story again. Fill in the missing key information in the notes below. Remember:

- Don't try to write down everything you hear. Write the important information only.
- Don't write complete sentences; write key words only.

▲ Bears are attracted to the smell of certain foods.

1. decided to go _____

2. weather was _____

3. after a half hour started to _____

4. hiked back to _____ to change _____

5. couldn't find _____

6. went back _____

7. saw _____ wearing _____

8. felt _____

9. problem now: _____

5 Summarizing Ideas

1. Compare your notes on the story with a partner. Summarize the story in your own words. As you speak, look at your notes to help you remember.

2. In groups of three, play the roles of the man, the woman, and the hotel manager from the story. Don't read the script. Use your notes to help you remember the story.

6 Reviewing Vocabulary Talk about the picture below. Use the new vocabulary as you describe what is happening.

Noun	Adjectives	Expression
hiking	clear	I can't wait to…
	incredible	
	muddy	
	scared	

Three hikers ▶

Talk It Over

7 Fact or Fiction Game

1. Tell the class about a dangerous, unusual, or exciting experience that you had in nature. Your teacher will give you a card. If the card says "Fact," you must tell a true story. If the card says "Fiction," tell an imaginary story, but make it sound true.

2. After each story, the class will take a vote: How many people think the story was fact? How many think it was fiction? See which student in your class is the best storyteller—or the most creative!

8 Role-Play Discuss the following questions.

1. What does the sign to the right mean? Why do you think camping areas and parks have signs like this?

2. Does your country have strong laws against littering (throwing paper and garbage on the ground or street)?

3. Why do you think some countries have strong laws against littering? How does litter affect the environment?

Culture Note

North America has many large, beautiful national parks. It is illegal to leave garbage in a park. It is also illegal to take plants or animals out of a park. Parks and camping areas always have **rangers**. Their job is to protect the parks and help park visitors.

> PLEASE TAKE
> NOTHING BUT
> PICTURES
> LEAVE NOTHING
> BUT FOOTPRINTS

▲ A common sign in U.S. parks

Look at the pictures below and read the description of the situation. In groups of three (George, Lou, and Rick), role-play the situation. The following expressions may help you express your ideas:

Explaining Rules

You need to…   It's against the rules to…

You shouldn't…   You're not allowed to…

George and Lou are brothers. They have just spent a wonderful weekend camping. Now they're getting ready to leave, but they are leaving their campsite dirty and full of trash. Rick is a park ranger. He stops the brothers to explain their responsibilities and to ask them to clean up. Make up your own ending.

Getting Meaning from Context

1 **Prelistening Questions** Before you listen, talk about the seasons with a partner.

1. Identify the seasons in the photos (winter, spring, summer, or fall) and describe the weather in each one.

2. Do you know of any countries that don't have four seasons? Describe the weather in those countries.

FOCUS ON TESTING

TOEFL® iBT

Using Context Clues

Many tests such as the TOEFL® iBT measure your academic listening and speaking abilities. This activity, and others in the book, will develop your social and academic communication abilities, and provide a foundation for success on a variety of standardized tests. You are going to hear five conversations about seasons. As you listen to each conversation, write *winter, spring, summer,* or *fall* in the **Seasons** column. After each conversation, stop the recording and write the words that helped you choose the season. Compare your answers and clues with a partner.

Seasons	Clues
1.	
2.	
3.	
4.	
5.	

Talk It Over

2 **Talking About Seasons** Talk with a partner about seasons in New York. Work in pairs: Student A and Student B. Follow the instructions below.

1. Student A, look at page 200, and Student B, look at page 204.
2. Ask your partner questions about the missing information in your chart.
3. Write your partner's answers in the blank spaces on your chart. When you finish, your charts should match.

Example

When is summer? OR What are the summer months?

What's the weather like in the spring?

Weather

1 **Listening for Temperatures** You will hear eight conversations about the weather. Circle the temperatures you hear in each conversation.

1.	19	95	99
2.	80	18	8
3.	13	30	30s
4.	14	40	44
5.	103	130	133
6.	30s	30	13
7.	−13	30	3
8.	70	70s	17

A thermometer ▶

> **Language Tip**
>
> Weather reports often say that the temperature is **in the 30s** (40s, 50s, etc.). **In the 30s** means that the temperature is anywhere between 30 and 39 degrees.

2 **Talking About Temperatures**
Your teacher will give each student the name of a city. Find today's temperatures around the world in a newspaper or online. Tell the class today's temperatures in the city your teacher gives you.

Example

Teacher: Sydney, Australia

Student: The high temperature will be 75 degrees Fahrenheit.
The low temperature will be 52.
Today's average temperature will be in the 70s.

3 **Previewing Vocabulary** Listen to the underlined words and phrases. You will hear the underlined words in a weather forecast. Write the letter of the correct definition beside each sentence.

Sentences

1. _____ Take an umbrella. There's a chance of showers later.

2. _____ Take a sweater. It's chilly outside.

3. _____ The overnight temperature will be 20 degrees.

4. _____ The sky is partly cloudy. It's not a good day for the beach.

5. _____ The weather forecast says we can expect fair skies this weekend. Let's go fishing!

Definitions

a. clear, not rainy

b. short periods of rain

c. during the night

d. clear in some places and cloudy in others

e. a little cold

4 **Listening to a Weather Forecast** Ming is watching the weather forecast. Listen to the report and use the chart to take notes about the weekend weather.

▲ A TV reporter giving a weather forecast

	Friday	Saturday	Sunday	Monday
Sky (Cloudy? Fair?):				
Temperature: High:				
Temperature: Low:				
Rain (Yes? No?):				

Work in groups of four. Each student summarizes the information for one day.

Example

Student 1: On Friday it will be partly cloudy with showers during the night.

Student 2: On Saturday…

FOCUS

Expressions for Talking About Activities You Like and Dislike

Likes	Dislikes
I like/love (*to+* verb/verb + *-ing*).	I don't like/dislike/hate (*to+* verb/ verb + *-ing*).
I enjoy (verb + *-ing*).	I'm not crazy about (noun).
It's OK/all right/fun/good /great/ wonderful.	I don't care for (noun).
I'm crazy about (noun).	It's awful/terrible.
	I can't stand it.

5 Interview Interview a partner about activities he or she likes or dislikes in each season. Complete the chart with your partner's answers.

Example

You ask: What do you like to do in the (summer)?
                      What's your favorite (winter) sport?
                      What activities do you dislike in (winter)?

Your partner answers: I like waterskiing in the summer.
                      My favorite winter activity is watching television!
                      I hate driving in the snow, but I enjoy making a snowman.

	Fall	Winter	Spring	Summer
Sports				
Other Activities (likes)				
Other Activities (dislikes)				

Self-Assessment Log

Check (✓) the words you learned in this chapter.

Nouns	Verb	Adjectives	Expressions
▦ chance of	▦ get a tan	▦ chilly	▦ couldn't wait (can't wait)
▦ degrees		▦ clear	▦ How come...?
▦ fair skies		▦ extra	▦ it's pouring (rain)
▦ fall		▦ freezing	
▦ hiking		▦ incredible	
▦ showers		▦ muddy	
▦ spring		▦ overnight	
▦ summer		▦ partly cloudy	
▦ weather forecast		▦ scared	
▦ winter		▦ sick of (verb + *-ing*)	

Check (✓) the things you did in this chapter. How well can you do each one?

	Very well	Fairly well	Not very well
I can listen to and practice stress and reductions.	☐	☐	☐
I can hear the difference between *can* and *can't*.	☐	☐	☐
I can talk about my abilities.	☐	☐	☐
I can take notes on a story.	☐	☐	☐
I can summarize my notes.	☐	☐	☐
I can guess meanings from context.	☐	☐	☐
I can talk about the weather.	☐	☐	☐
I can talk about my likes and dislikes.	☐	☐	☐

Write about what you learned and liked in this chapter.

In this chapter,

I learned _____

_____

I liked _____

_____

CHAPTER 3

Living to Eat, or Eating to Live?

"Tomatoes and oregano make it Italian; wine and tarragon make it French. Sour cream makes it Russian; lemon and cinnamon make it Greek. Soy sauce makes it Chinese; garlic makes it good."

Alice May Brock
American author

In this **CHAPTER**

Conversation Shopping for Food

Advice Show Healthy Eating

Getting Meaning from Context Eating Out

Real-World Tasks Following Recipes

Connecting to the Topic

1 Look at the photo. What are the people doing? What is their relationship to one another?

2 When do you eat with others? And who do you eat with?

3 Eating lots of vegetables is healthy. What are three other healthy eating habits?

Shopping for Food

Before You Listen

1 **Prelistening Questions**   Look at the photo. Answer the questions with a partner.

1. The supermarket in the picture has an "express line." What do you think this means?

2. There is a couple at the front of the line. What are they buying? What mistake do they make?

▲ Andrew and Nancy at the supermarket

2 Previewing Vocabulary Listen to these words and phrases from the conversation. Then complete the sentences with the words and phrases.

Nouns		Verb	Expression
aisle	produce	take checks	in line
groceries	quart[2]		
pound[1]	tofu[3]		

1. Cherries are pretty cheap now. They cost $1.89 a _____.

2. My son likes milk a lot. He drinks a _____ of milk every day.

3. You can pay with cash or a credit card, but this market doesn't

   _____.

4. I hate frozen or canned vegetables and fruit. I only eat fresh

   _____.

5. I just spent $90.00 on _____. Last time I spent $85.00.

   Food is really expensive here!

6. **A:** Excuse me, where is the bread?

   B: It's in _____ four.

7. The market was very crowded. I had to wait _____

   for 15 minutes to pay.

8. People who don't eat meat often cook with _____.

[1] 2.2 pounds equal one kilogram.
[2] A quart is equal to about a liter.
[3] Tofu is a soft white food made from soy beans, popular in Asian cooking.

Listen

3 Listening for Main Ideas Andrew and Nancy are grocery shopping at a supermarket. Close your book and listen. Prepare to answer these questions.

1. What are Andrew and Nancy discussing?

2. Why is Andrew buying so much food?

3. Why can't Andrew and Nancy use the express line?

Compare and discuss your answers with a partner.

4 Listening for Details Listen again if necessary. Write *T* if a statement is true and *F* if it is false. Correct the false statements.

1. _____ Andrew forgot to get tofu.

2. _____ Nancy wants Andrew to buy more ice cream.

3. _____ Strawberries cost $2.89.

Stress

5 **Listening for Stressed Words** Listen to the conversation again. Some of the stressed words are missing. During each pause, repeat the phrase or sentence. Then fill in the blanks with words you hear.

Andrew: Well, I got a few groceries that _____ on the list.

Nancy: I can _____ that! We're _____ shopping

for an _____, you know.

Andrew: I _____ do this when I'm hungry.

Nancy: Well, let's see what you _____ here.

Andrew: Some nice, fresh _____ for only _____
a pound.

Nancy: Well, that's fine. They always have nice _____ here.

But _____ do you have all these _____?

Andrew: Don't you _____ them?

Nancy: Oh, I don't know… I hope you got a _____ of

_____.

Andrew: I think I _____. Where's the _____ with

the Asian foods again?

Nancy: Aisle _____.

Andrew: I'll go get it.

Nancy: _____—this _____ you got looks really

_____!

Andrew: Well, it _____. It's on _____ for just

_____ a pound.

Nancy: And what's this? More ice cream? We already have a

_____ at home. Why don't you put it _____?

Meanwhile, I'll get in _____ right here.

Cashier: I'm _____, Miss; this is the _____ line, and

it looks like you've got more than _____ items. Oh,

and we don't take _____ here.

Now read the conversation with two other classmates. Practice stressing words correctly.

Reductions

6 **Comparing Unreduced and Reduced Pronunciation** The following sentences come from the conversation. Listen for the difference between unreduced and reduced pronunciation. Repeat both forms after the speaker.

Unreduced Pronunciation	Reduced Pronunciation*
1. Let's see what you have here.	Let's see whatcha have here.
2. Why do you have all these cookies?	Why d'ya have all these cookies?
3. Don't you like them?	Dontcha like 'em?
4. I don't know.	I dunno.

* Note: The underlined forms are not acceptable spellings in written English.

7 **Listening for Reductions** Listen to the following sentences. You'll hear the reduced pronunciations of some words. Repeat each sentence during the pause. Then write the unreduced forms of the missing words in the blanks.

Customer: Waiter?

Server: Yes, sir. Do you know _____ _____ want?

Customer: _____ _____ have the spaghetti with mushroom sauce tonight?

Server: Yes, we do.

Customer: Well, are the mushrooms fresh or canned?

Server: They're fresh, and the sauce has _____ _____ them.

Customer: Great, I'll have that.

Server: _____ _____ want something to drink?

Customer: I _____ _____. Why _____ _____ recommend something?

Server: How about some nice Italian mineral water?

With a partner, repeat the sentences for pronunciation practice. Practice reduced pronunciation.

8 **Using Vocabulary** Discuss the following questions with a partner. Use the underlined vocabulary in your answers.

1. Who shops for <u>groceries</u> in your family? How often?

2. What kinds of <u>produce</u> do you buy every week?

3. How much does a gallon (4 <u>quarts</u> = about 4 liters) of gasoline cost right now? Recently, has this price gone up, down, or stayed the same?

4. In your favorite food market, how many <u>aisles</u> are there?

5. About how many <u>pounds</u> (1 pound = about 1/2 kilogram) of groceries can you carry?

6. How do you feel when you have to stand <u>in line</u> for a long time?

Pronunciation

FOCUS

Teens or Tens?

Notice the differences in stress between the following pairs of words. In the numbers 13 to 19, be sure to stress the "-teen" ending. For 20, 30, 40, etc., to 90, stress the first syllable only. Listen.

thirteen′	thir′ty
fourteen′	for′ty
fifteen′	fif′ty
sixteen′	six′ty
seventeen′	sev′enty
eighteen′	eigh′ty
nineteen′	nine′ty

9 **Distinguishing Between Teens and Tens** Listen to the sentences and circle the number you hear.

1. 13   30   5. 17   70
2. 14   40   6. 18   80
3. 15   50   7. 19   90
4. 16   60

10 Listening for Teens and Tens Listen to these sentences. Write the number you hear on the blank line in each picture.

1.

2.

3.

4.

5.

6.

7.

8.

9.

10.

Talk It Over

11 Interview Use count and noncount nouns as you interview people about food and shopping habits.

1. Work in groups of three. Write your teacher's name and the names of your group members in the spaces at the top of the chart below.

2. Ask questions with "How much" or "How many" and the words on the left side of the chart. Look at the example (Stacy).

Example

A: How much coffee do you drink every day?

B: Two cups a day.

A: How many candy bars do you buy a week?

B: Two a week.

3. Practice asking your teacher the questions and write his or her answers on the chart.

- Use the present tense.
- Pay attention to count and noncount nouns.
- Add time expressions as needed. For example, "How much coffee do you drink *every week*?"

4. Take turns asking your group members the questions and write their answers on the chart.

> **Language Tip**
>
> Use **noncount nouns** to talk about food in a general way:
>
> I like ice cream.
> I'll have cereal.
> Steak is expensive.
>
> Use quantity words or container names to talk about specific amounts of food:
>
> - a quart (or gallon) of ice cream
> - a box of cereal
> - a pound of steak

> **Time Expressions you can use in the questions or answers:**
>
> each day/week/month
> every day/week/month
> a day/week/month

Key Words for Questions	Stacy	Teacher	Classmate 1	Classmate 2
coffee/drink	2 cups a day			
water/drink	6 glasses a day			
candy/buy	2			
food/eat/breakfast	Only a little			
money/spend/groceries	About 30 dollars			
gasoline/buy	About 15 gallons			
bananas/eat	3 or 4			
times/eat/restaurants	8 or 9			

Healthy Eating

Before You Listen

1 **Prelistening Questions** In the United States, people learn that they should eat food from the four major food groups: grains (wheat, corn, rice, etc.), fruits and vegetables, dairy (milk, cheese, yogurt, etc.), and protein (meat, fish, beans, nuts, eggs, etc.). Before you listen, answer these questions with a partner.

1. Talk about the photo. Are these students eating healthy food?

2. Do you eat like these students? For example, do you like "junk food"? If yes, what is your favorite type? If not, what kinds of food do you like to eat?

3. Do you ever eat canned or frozen food? Why or why not? If you do eat such foods, what are some examples?

4. Have you ever changed your eating habits (what, how much, or when you eat)? Explain how, and why, you changed your eating habits.

2 **Previewing Vocabulary** You will hear the underlined words below on a radio advice show. Listen to the underlined words. Then write the letter of the correct definition beside each sentence.

Sentences

1. _____ Milk is a good source of calcium.

2. _____ We can get most vitamins and minerals from food. We don't have to take pills.

3. _____ If you start to gain weight, you are probably eating more food than your body needs.

4. _____ If you skip breakfast, you'll be really hungry by lunchtime.

5. _____ Dentists try to teach children good brushing and eating habits so they won't get tooth decay.

6. _____ The doctor told John to cut down on coffee, to help him sleep better.

7. _____ A piece of bread has about 75 calories.

8. _____ Fiber helps food move through our bodies easily.

Definitions

a. weakening, rotting

b. a unit for measuring the energy value of food

c. to reduce or have less of (something)

d. a food substance that comes from plants and that we need for digestion

e. helpful elements in many foods that are used by our bodies to grow and stay healthy

f. not to do or have something

g. a place where something comes from

h. to increase

3 Listening for Main Ideas Listen to advice from a radio show called "Eating Right!" As you listen, answer this question:

What are some important things you can do to eat right?

4 Taking Notes on Specific Information Listen again. This time, complete the charts with Bob and Pam's advice. Try to catch as many details as you can.

Things You Should Eat	Reasons	Examples
vegetables	fiber,	carrots,

Things You Shouldn't Eat or Drink	Reasons	Examples

After You Listen

5 Summarizing Ideas

1. Compare your notes on the radio show with a partner. Together, summarize in complete sentences the advice you heard. Include reasons and examples. Tell your partner if you have tried any of the ideas for healthy eating.

   Example

   You should eat a carrot for a snack because it's a vegetable that has…

2. With your class, make a list on the board of additional dos and don'ts about healthy eating. Tell the class which ones you have tried and if they worked well.

6 **Using Vocabulary** Discuss the following questions with a partner. Use the underlined vocabulary in your answers.

1. Which meal are you least likely to <u>skip</u>, and which meal are you most likely to <u>skip</u>? Why?

2. Bodybuilders, football players, and other athletes often try to <u>gain</u> weight and strength. What specific types of food would you suggest for these people to eat?

3. What do you eat or drink that you know may be bad for your teeth? Would you consider stopping? Would you <u>cut down on</u> these things? How do you try to avoid tooth <u>decay</u>?

4. Do you ever think about the number of <u>calories</u> in certain foods you eat? Do you read food labels? Why or why not?

5. Which of your favorite foods do you think are the best <u>sources</u> of <u>vitamins and minerals</u>?

6. What kinds of foods do you eat to get <u>fiber</u> in your diet?

Talk It Over

7 **Comparing Eating Habits** "Eating habits" are your eating customs. They include when, where, and what you eat. Take notes in the chart below. Then use the chart to talk about differences between your eating habits at home and the way you eat when you travel somewhere.

	When I'm at Home	When I Travel
what you eat for breakfast, lunch, and dinner	I eat rice for breakfast.	I eat cereal for breakfast.
the time and size of meals and snacks		
the price of food		
restaurants		
table manners		

Getting Meaning from Context

1 Prelistening Questions Look at the photos. Each one shows a different kind of eating place. Before you listen, answer the questions on page 53 with a partner.

▼ A cafeteria

▼ A restaurant

◄ A fast-food restaurant

▲ A customer gets take out food at a diner.

1. What kind of food does each place serve?

2. Who serves the food in each place?

3. Which place is probably the most expensive? Which is the cheapest?

4. When would you choose to eat in each kind of place?

5. Which of these kinds of places have you tried?

6. What are some other types of places to eat?

FOCUS ON TESTING

Using Context Clues

Many tests such as the TOEFL® iBT measure your academic listening and speaking abilities. This activity, and others in the book, will develop your social and academic communication abilities, and provide a foundation for success on a variety of standardized tests. You will hear four conversations about places to eat.

1. Listen to the beginning of each conversation.

2. Listen to the question for each conversation. Stop the recording and choose the best answer to each question.

3. In the **Clues** column, write the words that helped you choose your answer.

4. Listen to the last part of each conversation to hear the correct answer.

Answers	Clues
1. (A) coffee shop (B) cafeteria (C) nice restaurant	
2. (A) fast-food place (B) diner (C) expensive restaurant	
3. (A) cafeteria (B) coffeehouse (C) fast-food place	
4. (A) nice restaurant (B) cafeteria (C) fast-food place	

Ordering in a Restaurant

In the United States, you can order dinner *à la carte*, which means you pay separately for each item. You can also order a complete dinner, which includes a main course (fish, meat, or a vegetarian dish), soup or salad, and side dishes (rice, potatoes, or vegetables) for one price. Drinks and dessert are usually separate. A *dish* in this context is a serving of cooked food, not a container.

Here is a list of questions and answers that are frequently used in restaurants.

Server	Customer
Taking an order: Are you ready to order? May I take your order? Do you want (an appetizer)? Would you like (soup) or (salad)? Would you prefer (French fries) or (a baked potato)? What would you like (to drink)?	*Ordering:* I'll have (the beans and rice). I'd like (a steak). May I please have (a glass of iced tea)? *Asking for information:* Do you have (tofu)? What kind of (salad dressing) do you have? Does that come with (a vegetable)?

2 Ordering in a Restaurant A customer is ordering a meal at a nice restaurant. Listen to the conversation.

Server: Are you ready to order, ma'am?

Customer: Yes, I am.

Server: What would you like?

Customer: I'd like the grilled salmon dinner.

Server: Would you like soup or salad with that?

Customer: What kind of soup do you have?

Server: We have Japanese miso soup or Italian minestrone.

Customer: I'll have the minestrone.

Server: And would you like potatoes or rice with your salmon?

Customer: Rice, please. Does the dinner come with a vegetable?

Server: Yes. Would you prefer green beans or broccoli?

Customer: Green beans, please.

Server: What would you like to drink?

Customer: I'd like a glass of iced tea.

Server: OK, that's minestrone soup, followed by grilled salmon with rice and green beans, and a glass of iced tea. Would you like an appetizer while you're waiting?

Customer: No thanks. But may I please have a glass of water?

Server: Of course. I'll bring it right out.

Customer: Thank you.

Now use the model conversation to role-play ordering dinner. Sit with a partner. One of you is the server. The other is a customer. Follow the instructions in the boxes below.

Server's Instructions

Start by asking the customer, "May I take your order?"

Then take the customer's order for a main course, soup or salad, side dishes, dessert, and a drink.

Customer's Instructions

Order the following items from the menu:

- a main course
- soup or salad
- a side dish
- dessert
- a drink

Ask questions about each course.

For example, "What kind of juice do you have?" "Is the shrimp fresh?"

Dinner Menu

SOUPS
Soup of the Day $3.25
Cheese Soup $3.50
Homemade Chili $3.75

SALADS
American Chef $7.25
Garden greens with turkey, ham, cheese

Golden Gate $7.75
Fresh pineapple stuffed with almond chicken salad

Tutti–Fruiti............................... $7.75
Fresh fruits served with cottage cheese

SIDE ORDERS
French Fries $3.50

Mushrooms $4.25
Covered in cheese sauce

Mixed Vegetables.................... $4.25
Steamed or stir-fried

HOUSE SPECIALTIES
All entrées served with your choice of rice, cottage cheese, tossed salad, choice of potato, roll and butter.

Ribeye Steak $15.75
Grilled to order

Whole Chicken $14.75
Broiled, baked, or fried

Sesame Tofu $13.95
Sautéed with snow peas and scallions

Fantail Shrimp $17.95
Broiled with butter and lemon, or deep fried

DESSERTS
Apple Pie $4.75
Plenty of cinnamon and a scoop of ice cream

Ice Cream $3.75
Or your choice of low-fat yogurt

BEVERAGES
Fresh juices $2.50
Cola & Diet Cola $1.20
Milk...$1.50

Recipes and Regional Foods

Recipes

1 **Previewing Vocabulary** The following words are used in cooking. Before you listen, write the definitions of the words.

ingredients:_____

serve: _____

beat: _____

melt: _____

dip: _____

fry: _____

Culture Note

Cooking Measurements
The measurements used in cooking in the United States are different from the measurements used in other countries.

For example:

United States	Other Countries
a teaspoon	= 5 ml (milliliters)
a tablespoon	= 15 ml
a cup	= 240 ml

2 **Taking Notes on a Recipe** Tom is teaching Kenji how to cook French toast. Listen to the recipe and take notes in the spaces below and on the next page.

Ingredients:_____

_____

_____

_____

_____

1.

2.

3.

Steps:

1. Beat _____

2. Melt _____

3. Dip _____

4.

5.

4. Fry _____

5. Serve _____

3 **Explaining a Recipe** Now, with a partner, use your notes to take turns explaining how to make French toast.

4 **Sharing Recipes** Teach the class a simple recipe for a dish that you know how to cook.

1. First, list the ingredients.

2. Then, describe each step (you may even try to demonstrate). As you speak, the class should take notes on the ingredients and steps.

3. Then, choose one or two people to retell the recipe using their notes.

Regional Foods

▲ Sushi

5 **Prelistening Questions** Before you listen, talk about "foreign" foods with a partner.

1. Do you know of any regions or places famous for special kinds of food? Give examples, and try to describe those foods.

2. Can you name some foreign foods and the countries they come from? Which foreign dishes have you tasted? What is your favorite?

3. Have you tried any North American food? What have you tried?

▲ Enchiladas with rice and beans

6 Regional Foods Andrew and Nancy plan to drive around the United States and Canada. Their friend, Paula, is a chef. She tells them about foods and drinks that are popular in different regions. Look at the map of the United States and Canada. As you hear the name of each food, write it on the map in the place where it is popular.

Discuss these questions with a partner.

1. Have you visited any of the cities or states mentioned by Paula? Did you eat any of the foods mentioned?

2. Which of the foods that Paula mentions would you like to try?

▲ Chinese food

▲ lobster

◄ Japanese food

Talk It Over

7 Refusing Food Politely

1. Read the situation in the box below and answer the question.

Has something like this ever happened to you?

> A Korean student, Soo Yun, is having dinner at the home of her American friend, Cathy. Soo Yun has only eaten American food a few times before. During the meal, Cathy's mother offers Soo Yun some unfamiliar food. Soo Yun prefers not to eat it, but she doesn't want to be rude. What can she do?

2. Prepare the conversation between Soo Yun and Cathy's mother with a partner. Put on a skit for the class. You can use the expressions below. After each skit, discuss whether or not the food was refused politely.

Offering Food to Someone	Refusing Food Politely
Would you like some _____?	Thanks, but I'm getting full.
Would you like to try some _____?	Thanks, but I've had enough.
Why don't you have some (more) _____?	I'm really full, but thanks.
Have some (more) _____.	It's delicious, but I really can't eat any more.
	It looks wonderful, but I can't eat any more.

Self-Assessment Log

Check (✓) the words you learned in this chapter.

Nouns
- aisle
- calories
- decay
- fiber
- groceries
- ingredients
- pound
- produce
- quart
- source
- tofu
- vitamins and minerals

Verbs
- beat
- cut down on
- dip
- fry
- gain
- melt
- serve
- skip
- take checks

Expression
- in line

Check (✓) the things you did in this chapter. How well can you do each one?

	Very well	Fairly well	Not very well
I can listen to and practice stress and reductions.	☐	☐	☐
I can hear the difference between tens and teens.	☐	☐	☐
I can talk about food, recipes, and eating habits.	☐	☐	☐
I can take notes on a radio advice show.	☐	☐	☐
I can summarize my notes.	☐	☐	☐
I can guess meanings from context.	☐	☐	☐
I can order food from a menu.	☐	☐	☐

Write what you learned and liked in this chapter.

In this chapter,

I learned _____

_____

I liked _____

_____

4 In the Community

> Without a sense
> of caring, there
> can be no sense
> of community.
>
> Anthony J. D'Angelo

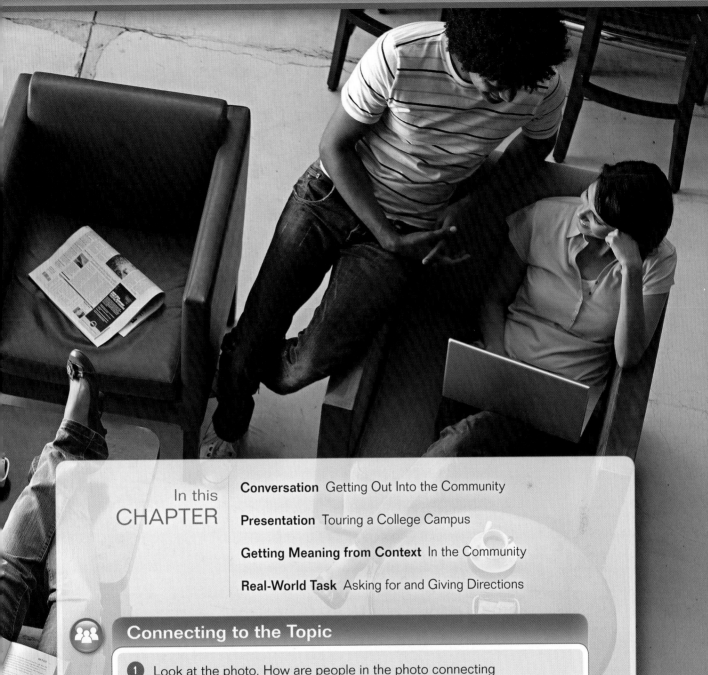

In this CHAPTER

Conversation Getting Out Into the Community

Presentation Touring a College Campus

Getting Meaning from Context In the Community

Real-World Task Asking for and Giving Directions

Connecting to the Topic

1. Look at the photo. How are people in the photo connecting with other people?

2. Phones, e-mail, texting, Facebook, Twitter, and spending time together are some ways to stay in touch. What do you like or dislike most about each example?

3. How do you communicate with your friends and family? Name all of the ways.

Getting Out Into the Community

1 **Prelistening Questions**   Answer the questions in small groups. Then, share with the class.

1. How much time do you spend online? Do you know anyone who spends too much time online? Describe.

2. What are some fun activities or events you can enjoy in the community where you live or study?

3. Have you, or anyone you know, done volunteer work to help other people, such as children, foreigners, the poor, the sick, or the elderly?

4. If you could do something to volunteer to improve your community, what would it be? Why?

2 **Previewing Vocabulary**   Listen to these words and phrases from the conversation. Then complete the sentences on page 65 with the words and phrases from the box.

Words and Phrases	Definitions
(be) supposed to	People think or expect something will happen
do community service	Help people who need it: homeless, poor, sick, old
ethnic (food)	Interesting/unusual foreign, international (food)
lose/lost track of time	To forget how much time is passing
See what I mean?	Here is a good example of my point, I told you so
shelter	A home or house for people who need it
show up	To arrive, appear
sign up	To put your name on a list because you want to join an activity, club, or group
sounds good	I think that's a good idea
to "get out"	To leave your home to meet people or do fun things
tons of stuff	A lot of things
volunteering	Giving your time to help others, without pay

1. I'm sorry I'm late. I was playing video games online and I guess I _____ time.

2. Whenever I see you, you're always at home on your phone or your laptop. You need to _____ more and make some new friends in town.

3. Wow! Look at the calendar for the summer music festival. There is _____ to listen to.

4. **A:** I'm glad you asked me to that party last night. The people were really nice.
   B: _____? It was much better than staying home alone with your Xbox!

5. Berkeley has so many _____ restaurants to choose from; last night I had delicious Chinese noodle soup, and tonight we're going out for Mexican tacos, or maybe Indian curry.

6. **A:** Do you want me to introduce you to my sister? I think you'd like her.
   B: Sure, _____. Let's all go out for coffee this weekend.

7. After I finish college this summer, I really want to _____ _____ at a hospital. I don't want the pay, I just want to help people.

8. _____ is very satisfying. When I spend the weekend doing that, I get back so much love from the people I try to help.

9. I'm so happy the city added 50 beds to the homeless _____. Now most of the people living on the street can sleep somewhere warm and safe.

10. Don't just _____ at your neighbor's apartment without calling first. He might be sleeping.

11. Jim Carrey's new movie _____ be very funny; let's go see it next weekend.

12. I think you should _____ to join the hip-hop dance class. You always wanted to do it–get on the list before it's too late.

3 **Listening for Main Ideas** Peter and Kenji are talking about getting out in the community this weekend. Close your book as you listen to the conversation. Listen for the answers to these questions. Then, discuss your answers with the class.

1. What does Peter advise Kenji to do more often? Why?

2. What kinds of things can Kenji and Peter do in their free time in the community?

3. How does Kenji feel about Peter's idea to do community service?

4 **Listening for Details** Listen again if necessary. Write *T* if a statement is true and *F* if it is false. Correct the false statements.

1. _____ Kenji has many ideas about fun places and things to do in the town.

2. _____ Kenji was able to see the free concert last Saturday on his computer.

3. _____ Peter is planning to go to the street festival downtown on Sunday.

Stress

5 **Listening for Stressed Words** Listen to the conversation again. Some of the stressed words are missing. During each pause, repeat the phrase or sentence. Then fill in the blanks with words you hear.

Peter: Dude, you _____ have the computer on? You've been here on Facebook and Skype for _____!

Kenji: I'm just _____ with some friends. I guess I _____ track of time.

Peter: Yeah, you're online _____ too much. You've got to get _____ more. It'll help your _____.

Kenji: To tell you the _____, I'm not sure where to go. I'm still kind of _____ here. And I have to study!

Peter: Well, there is _____ of _____ to do in town.

Kenji: Like what?

Peter: Like the free _____ in the park last Saturday, and...

Kenji: Oh. I watched some of it on _____.

Peter: See what I _____? You're not going to meet _____ that way! Come hang out with us more.

Kenji: OK, what are you guys doing _____ weekend?

Peter: There is this street festival _____. It's supposed to

have some _____ ethnic food, some _____,

and an art show. We're going to _____ our bikes there.

Kenji: Sounds good. Saturday or Sunday?

Peter: Actually, it's _____ days. But we're going to go on

Saturday because Sunday we're doing community _____.

Kenji: _____ service? You mean like volunteering?

Peter: Yeah. That's another thing you should do with us. We

_____ at a homeless shelter twice a _____.

It's really cool because we get to help _____ and meet some

interesting people at the same time.

Kenji: Hmm... I might be _____ in that. Can I just show

_____?

Peter: Yeah, I _____ so, but first sign up online. The

_____ is www.volunteer.com. Just don't stay on the

_____ forever...

Kenji: Man, you sound just like my _____. Okay, I'll study a bit
more, then look up that link.

Reductions

6 **Comparing Unreduced and Reduced Pronunciation** The following
sentences come from the conversation. Listen for the difference between
unreduced and reduced pronunciation. Repeat both forms after the speaker.

Unreduced Pronunciation	**Reduced Pronunciation***
1. I guess I lost track of time.	I guess I lost tracka time.
2. You've got to get out more.	You gotta gedout more.
3. I'm still kind of new here.	I'm still kinda new here.
4. Well, there's tons of stuff to do in town.	Well, there's tonsa stuff to do in town.
5. Supposed to have some great ethnic food...	Sposta have some great ethnic food...
6. We're going to ride our bikes there.	We're gonna ride our bikes there.
7. Can I just show up?	Can I jushow up?

* Note: The underlined forms are not acceptable spellings in written English.

7 **Listening for Reductions** Listen to the following conversation. You'll hear the reduced pronunciation of some words. Repeat each sentence during the pause. Then write the unreduced forms of the missing words in the blanks.

A: So I hear you're _____ _____ study in the U.S.—in Los Angeles, right?

B: Yeah. I'm excited! There 's _____ _____ stuff to do

there. You _____ _____ _____ come

visit me.

A: OK, I'll _____ _____ up at your door one

day and surprise you.

B: Great… Oh wow it's late. Let's _____

_____ _____ here. We're _____

_____ meet Anshu for dinner in ten minutes.

A: Sorry I got here late—I _____ _____

_____ _____ _____ time.

B: No problem. We can catch a taxi.

8 **Reductions Game**

Scenario 1: Pretend that a fire is moving toward the community you live in. You have 10 minutes to get out of your home and move to safety. Follow the steps to tell what you are going to do:

1. Sit in a circle. (or several circles – the more students in the circle, the more challenging the game). The first student says one thing he or she is going to do. Use the reduced forms and the words from the Word Bank section in the box on page 69.

   Example

   Student 1: I'm <u>gonna</u> save my dog.

2. The next student repeats the first student's sentence and then adds his or her own sentence.

   Example

   Student 2: She's <u>gonna</u> save her dog, and I <u>hafta</u> take my iPhone.

3. The third student repeats the first two sentences, and adds his or her own, and so on. Continue around the group until someone can't correctly remember all of the sentences. This student is out of the game.

4. Give the next student a chance to say everything correctly, and add a new sentence. Continue the game, adding one action each time, until there is only one student who can correctly remember all of the sentences. This is the winner.

Reductions

have to	hafta	going to	gonna	got to	gotta
has to	hasta	want to	wanna	because	'cause

Word Bank Scenario 1

Nouns

		Verbs	
brother/sister	family photos	call	save
clothes	jewelry	find	take
computer/cell phone	money	look for	turn off the gas/electricity
dog/cat/bird/pet	TV/books	rescue	warn

After You Listen

9 **Using Vocabulary** Answer the following questions in groups of three. One member asks the others the question. Each time the other two students answer using the underlined vocabulary, they get a point. (No vocabulary = no points.) Rotate the score keeper for each question. The student with the most points wins the game.

be supposed to	lose/lost track of time	sign up
do community services	See what I mean?	sounds good
ethnic (food)	shelter	tons of stuff
get out	show up	volunteering

Example

Student 1:   What happens if you lose track of time during a test?

Student 2:   If I lose track of time, I can't finish the test. (1 point)

Student 3:   I will fail the test. (0 points)

1. What happens if you lose track of time during a test?

2. Did you have tons of stuff to do last weekend? Why or why not?

3. If someone says, "See what I mean?," what are some possible answers? Discuss.

4. What are some of your favorite ethnic foods? Explain.

5. Give some ideas about things to do this weekend so your partner can respond with "Sounds good."

6. Did you ever do community service in your country? Explain. If not, what community service would you like to try?

7. Is <u>volunteering</u> part of any high school or university program in your home community?

8. In what kinds of emergencies do people need to find <u>shelter</u>?

9. In your country, can you just <u>show up</u> at a doctor's office, or do you need to make an appointment? How about at a restaurant?

10. Why do you need to be careful when you <u>sign up</u> for an online community, such as a dating service or discussion group?

11. Do you know what the weather is <u>supposed to be</u> like tomorrow?

Using Language Functions

FOCUS

Describing Locations

The following expressions are often used to describe locations in a community.

- on _____
  name of street
- near
- nearby
- next to
- next door to
- in front of
- across from / across the street from
- at the corner of _____ and _____
  street   street
- 2, 3, 4… blocks from
- in the middle of the block

Finding Locations Work with a partner. Look at the picture of a street scene. Decide if the sentences under the picture are correct or incorrect. If the location is wrong, make the necessary correction. Use expressions from the "Describing Locations" section on page 70.

Example

A: The In Hotel is across from the coffee shop with free wifi.

B: No, that's wrong. The In Hotel is across from Moon Books.

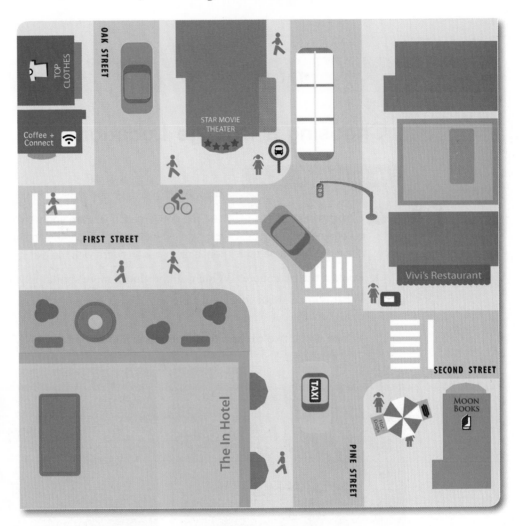

1. Vivi's Restaurant is in the middle of the block.

2. The woman buying a hot dog is standing in front of the park.

3. The bus stop is near the movies.

4. The bike rider is at the corner of First and Oak Street.

5. Star Movie Theater is next to a cafe with free wifi.

6. The mailbox is across the street from the movie theater.

7. The park is in front of Moon Books.

8. Top Clothes is next door to a coffee shop with free wifi.

11 Describing Your Neighborhood Describe your neighborhood to a partner. What kind of buildings, stores, and facilities are nearby? Use the expressions from page 70.

Example

I live in a very nice neighborhood. Everything I need is nearby. There is a market just three blocks from my house. And the neighbors across the street are...

PART 2 Conversation

Choosing a College Location

Before You Listen

1 Prelistening Questions The conversation you are about to hear is about college neighborhoods. Before you listen, look at the photos and answer the questions with a partner. Then, share your answers with the class.

1. Look at the two photos. Which campus looks more similar to your school?
2. What is good about college in a big city? What is good about college in a small town?
3. Which of the two colleges in the photos would you prefer? Why?

▲ Borough of Manhattan Community College

▲ The University of Montana

2 Previewing Vocabulary You will hear the underlined words below in a conversation. Listen to the underlined words. Then write the letter of the correct definition beside each sentence.

Sentences

1. _____ Los Angeles has a diverse population, including many Asians, African-Americans, and Latin-Americans.

2. _____ Urban areas have lots of excitement as well as heavy traffic and big crowds.

3. _____ Rosa was born in Brazil, but her background is Japanese.

4. _____ Everybody knows Seoul National University's high academic reputation.

5. _____ Music and television are too distracting when I study. I can only focus in complete quiet.

6. _____ We don't have a washing machine at home, so we go to a laundromat once a week.

7. _____ The high cost of housing is one downside to living in a big city.

Definitions

a. related to education

b. different types of

c. city

d. negative part, disadvantage

e. person's family history

f. interrupting, taking away attention

g. a place to clean clothes

Listen

3 Listening for Main Ideas Jessie is giving a tour of her college. As you listen, decide what the main idea of the conversation is. Then answer the question below.

What is the best title for this conversation?

Ⓐ Choosing the Right College

Ⓑ College Location: Big City or Small Town?

Ⓒ Why You Should Study in a Small Town

Ⓓ The Good and Bad of Studying in a Large City

Strategy

Graphic Organizer: Concept Map

A concept map can help you organize your notes when a speaker is comparing two or more sides of a topic. You can also use a concept map to organize your own ideas when you are comparing two or more sides of a topic.

 4 **Taking Notes on Specific Information** Listen again. Write the key words in the blanks.

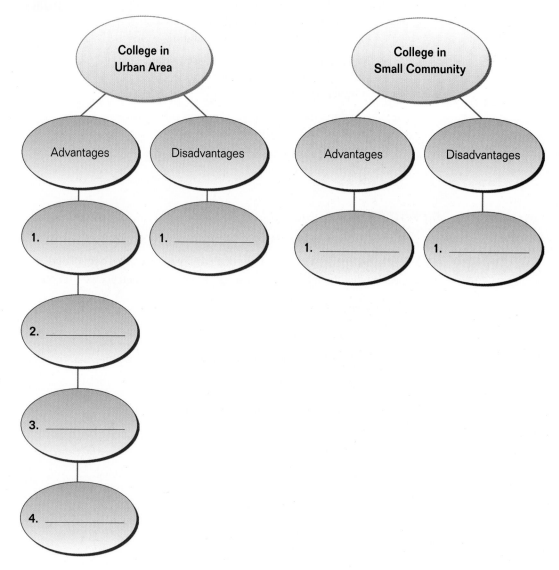

College in Urban Area

Advantages

1. _____

2. _____

3. _____

4. _____

Disadvantages

1. _____

College in Small Community

Advantages

1. _____

Disadvantages

1. _____

5 Summarizing Ideas Compare your notes with a partner. Using the keywords from your notes, summarize orally what Jessie said.

Example

Jessie talked about why she chose a college in a big city. First, she likes that...

 6 Using Vocabulary Discuss your answers to the following questions with a partner. Use the underlined vocabulary in your answers.

1. What's another underline{downside} to studying in a large city?
2. What universities in your country have the best academic reputation? Which ones are located in, or outside of, urban environments?
3. What things are most distracting for students who live and study in a dormitory?
4. Do you prefer to live in a community with a diverse population? Or do you prefer to live with people from similar backgrounds? Why?
5. What's your favorite ethnic restaurant? Describe.

PART 3 Strategies for Better Listening and Speaking

Getting Meaning from Context

FOCUS ON TESTING

Using Context Clues

Many tests such as the TOEFL® iBT measure your academic listening and speaking abilities. This activity, and others in the book, will help develop your social and academic communication abilities and provide a foundation for success on a variety of standardized tests. You are going to hear five conversations from different places in the city.

1. Listen to the beginning of each conversation.
2. Listen to the question for each conversation. Stop the recording and choose the best answer to each question.
3. In the clues column, write the words that helped you choose your answer.
4. Listen to the last part of each conversation to hear the correct answer.

Answers	Clues

1. Where are the speakers?
    Ⓐ bus station
    Ⓑ subway station
    Ⓒ getting into a taxi	

2. Where are the speakers?
    Ⓐ coffee shop
    Ⓑ computer store
    Ⓒ hotel room	

3. Where are the speakers?
    Ⓐ cafeteria
    Ⓑ supermarket
    Ⓒ farmers' market	

4. Where are the speakers?
    Ⓐ at a clothing store
    Ⓑ at a laundromat
    Ⓒ at a gas station	

5. Who is the man talking to?
    Ⓐ an eye doctor
    Ⓑ a tailor
    Ⓒ a hairstylist	

Asking for and Giving Directions

Using Language Functions

FOCUS

Expressions for Asking for and Giving Directions

You will listen to Jessie giving directions to different places near campus. Before you listen, study the expressions listed below.

Asking for Directions	Giving Directions
Could you tell me where… is? Where is…? Do you know how to get to…? How do I get to…? I'm looking for… I'm trying to find…	Go straight. Go straight for two blocks on (Lennox) Avenue/Street/Road. Go past (the market). Go north/south/east/west. Turn right/left. Make a right/left. Cross the street. You'll see it on your right/left.

▲ "Excuse me, I'm looking for the Student Center."

1 **Reading a Map** Look at the map below. For each item, choose a place to start. Then, choose a place to end. Write directions on the lines. Then say your directions to your group. The group will guess your starting and ending places.

1. From _____ to _____.

Directions _____

_____

_____

2. From _____ to _____.

Directions _____

_____

_____

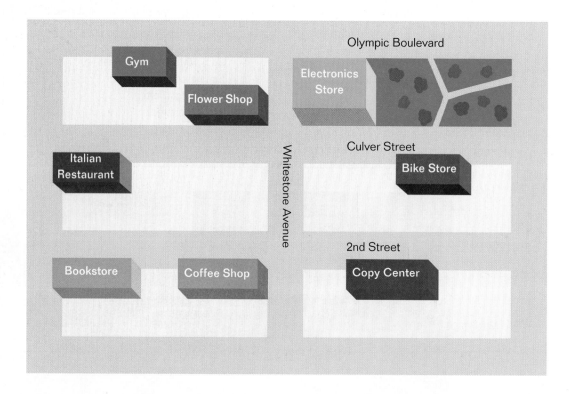

2 **Following Directions** Jessie is finished with the campus tour. Visitors are asking her for directions to different places in the neighborhood. Right now they are standing at the corner of Le Conte Avenue and Westwood Boulevard in Los Angeles.

1. Find the X at Le Conte Ave and Westwood Blvd on the map.

2 Listen to directions and follow them on the map. Start at the corner of Le Conte and Westwood.

3. Find and write the name of each place the visitors are looking for.

Ⓐ _____

Ⓑ _____

Ⓒ _____

Ⓓ _____

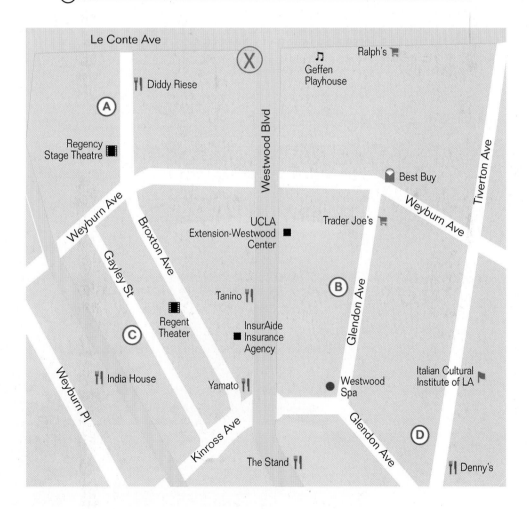

③ Getting Directions Listen to the following conversations about directions. Take notes on each conversation.

1. Place to get on: _____

   Bus Number: _____   How often it runs _____

   Bus fare: $ _____

   Place to get off: _____

   Destination: _____

2. Destination: _____

   First subway train, Number: _____

   Direction: _____

   Change at : _____ Station

   Second subway train, Number: _____

   Direction: _____

   Station to get off: _____

3. Start at: _____ Get on Air Train: _____ Line

   Get off at: _____

   Change to a: _____ train, ONLY going to: _____

   Get off at (destination): _____

▲ A man studies the Washington, D.C. subway map.

Self-Assessment Log

Check (✓) the words you learned in this chapter.

Nouns	Verbs	Expressions	Adjectives
▨ background	▨ get out	▨ See what I mean?	▨ academic
▨ community service	▨ lose track of time	▨ Sounds good.	▨ distracting
▨ downside	▨ show up		▨ diverse
▨ laundromat	▨ sign up for		▨ ethnic
▨ shelter	▨ volunteer		▨ urban
▨ tons of stuff	▨ be supposed to		
▨ volunteering			

Check (✓) the things you did in this chapter. How well can you do each one?

	Very well	Fairly well	Not very well
I can listen to and practice stress and reductions.	☐	☐	☐
I can take notes on a conversation.	☐	☐	☐
I can summarize my notes.	☐	☐	☐
I can guess meanings from context.	☐	☐	☐
I can describe locations.	☐	☐	☐
I can use a concept map.	☐	☐	☐
I can follow directions on a map.	☐	☐	☐
I can listen to, ask for, and give directions.	☐	☐	☐

Write what you learned and liked in this chapter.

In this chapter,

I learned _____

_____

I liked _____

_____

5 Home

Home is a place
you grow up wanting
to leave, and grow
old wanting to get
back to.

John Ed Pearce
Journalist

In this
CHAPTER

Conversation Renting an Apartment

Presentation Student Housing Choices

Getting Meaning from Context Conversations About Housing

Real-World Task Housing Exchange

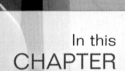

Connecting to the Topic

1 What are the people in the picture doing?

2 How many times have you moved to a new home? What were your reasons for moving?

3 Do young adults in your culture often live separately from their families? Why or why not?

Renting an Apartment

Before You Listen

1 **Prelistening Questions** Before you listen, talk with a partner.

1. What kind of place do you live in now: an apartment? A house? A student dormitory?

2. Look at the photo and the housing ad.

- What useful information is missing from the ad?
- What questions does the woman probably have about this apartment?
- What questions might the manager ask her?

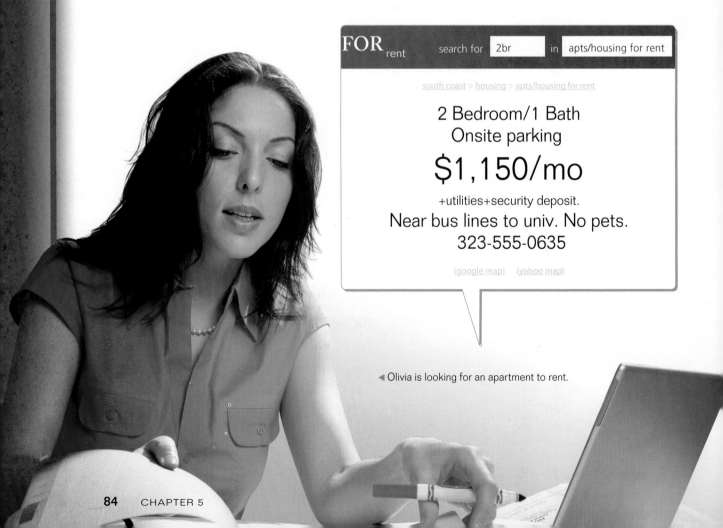

FOR rent   search for   2br   in   apts/housing for rent

south coast > housing > apts/housing for rent

2 Bedroom/1 Bath
Onsite parking

$1,150/mo

+utilities+security deposit.
Near bus lines to univ. No pets.
323-555-0635

(google map)   (yahoo map)

◄ Olivia is looking for an apartment to rent.

2 Previewing Vocabulary Listen to the words and phrases from the conversation. Then complete the sentences below with the correct form of the words and phrases.

Nouns	Verb	Adjectives
bus line	require	available
landlord		on-site
laundry		refundable
security deposit		unfurnished
unit		

1. I don't need a car because there are three _____ near my house.

2. When I take a bus, the driver _____ that I pay only by cash.

3. Our office building has no _____ parking. We have to park our cars several blocks away.

4. My apartment manager is so busy, he is never _____ when I need him.

5. Nancy's building has no _____, so she bought a washing machine for her _____.

6. The price of a movie ticket is not _____, so you can't get your money back if you don't like the movie.

7. Ming and her roommate have to buy beds, tables and chairs because their apartment is _____.

8. Does your _____ become angry if you don't pay your rent on time?

9. When we moved out of our apartment, we got back our $1000 _____ because we left the apartment clean and undamaged.

Listen

3 Listening for Main Ideas Olivia is calling about an apartment for rent. Close your books and listen to the conversation. Listen for the answer to these questions.

1. Who is this apartment for?

2. What is required before moving into this apartment?

3. What information does Olivia learn that is not in the ad?

4. At the end of the conversation, what does Olivia decide to do?

4 **Listening for Details** Listen again if necessary. Write *T* if a statement is true and *F* if it is false. Then compare with a partner and correct the false information.

1. _____ This apartment is close to campus.

2. _____ The apartment is furnished.

3. _____ Olivia can do her laundry in the building.

4. _____ A cleaning fee is required before moving in.

Stress

5 **Listening for Stressed Words** Listen to the conversation again. Some of the stressed words are missing. During each pause, repeat the phrase or sentence. Then fill in the blanks with words you hear.

Manager (Mgr): Hello?

Olivia: Hi. My _____ is Olivia. I'm _____ about the _____ for rent.

Mgr: Oh, yes. Which one?

Olivia: The _____ bedroom one bath for _____.

Mgr: OK. That one is still _____.

Olivia: I see. It's _____, right?

Mgr: Right.

Olivia: Can you _____ me a little _____ about it? Like, uh, where is it _____?

Mgr: We're at National Boulevard and Bundy. Did you see our _____ online?

Olivia: Yes, on Craigslist. It says you're _____ bus lines—that's good, 'cause I go to _____ every day.

Mgr: Oh, so you're a _____ student. How many _____ is this for?

Olivia: Just me and my _____. Um, can you tell me, is there _____ on-site?

Mgr: Yes, there's on-site _____, just not in the unit though. We have a laundry room _____. It's a very nice building, _____ entrance, elevator, you've got a nice view of the _____...

Olivia: That's good. What kind of _____ do you require?

Mgr: Well, I can _____ you an application; it

_____ everything. But the main thing we require is

one-month _____ as a security deposit and a

_____ cleaning fee—that's _____

refundable. And of course we _____ a credit check.

Olivia: Oh, I see. Well, my roommate and I are _____

students, so I'm not _____ about the _____.

Mgr: Well, you know what? Don't _____ about that right

now. Why don't you _____ _____ and

see the place. I'm here _____ to _____

every day.

Olivia: OK, we can come by _____ today, around 4:30.

Can you give me the _____ address?

Mgr: 5443 National. And your _____ was Olivia, right?

Olivia: Right. Olivia Sandoval. Are you the _____?

Mgr: No, I'm the _____. I'm Larry. My

_____ is next to the front door.

Olivia: OK, I'll _____ you later then.

Mgr: See you _____. Bye.

Now read the conversation with a partner. Practice stressing words correctly.

Reductions

6 **Comparing Unreduced and Reduced Pronunciation** The following sentences come from the conversation. Listen for the difference between unreduced and reduced pronunciation. Repeat both forms after the speaker.

Unreduced Pronunciation	Reduced Pronunciation*
1. Did you see our ad online?	Didja see our ad online?
2. What kind of deposit do you require?	What kinda deposit do you require?
3. You've got a nice view of the park.	You've got a nice view uh'the park.
4. I can email you an application.	I 'kn email you an application.
5. Why don't you come by and see the place?	Why doncha come by 'n see the place?
6. Can you give me the exact address?	Canya gimme the exact address?
7. I'll see you later then.	I'll seeya later then.

*Note: The underlined forms are not acceptable spellings in written English.

7 Listening for Reductions Listen to the following conversation. You'll hear the reduced pronunciations of some words. Repeat each sentence during the pause. Then write the unreduced forms of the missing words in the blanks.

Steve: Uh-oh. I can't find my keys.

Margot: What _____ _____ keys? House keys?

Steve: Yeah.

Margot: _____ _____ have an extra one?

Steve: Yeah, but not with me. I gave an extra key to _____ _____ _____ neighbors.

Margot: OK, then you _____ get _____ keys from him.

Steve: No, _____ he's on vacation.

Margot: Then you're _____ _____ need to call a locksmith.

Steve: OK, _____ _____ your phone.

Margot: Why? _____ _____ lose your phone too?

Steve: No, it's locked in the house.

With a partner, read the conversation. Practice reduced pronunciation.

After You Listen

8 Using Vocabulary Work in pairs. Quiz your partner on the new vocabulary from the conversation. Student A should look at page 201. Student B should look at page 205. Follow the instructions.

Pronunciation

FOCUS

The -ed Ending in Past Tense Verbs

The -ed ending in past tense verbs is pronounced one of three ways, depending on the sound that comes before -ed.

/id/ after -d and -t

Examples waited, invited, needed

/t/ after unvoiced sounds: -p, -k, -f, -s, -ch, -sh, -x

Examples missed, watched, helped

/d/ after vowels and other voiced sounds: -b, -g, -j, -m, -n, -l, -r, -th, -v, -z, -w

Examples lived, showed, listened

9 **Distinguishing Among -ed Endings** Listen and write the following words. Then check the sound you hear at the end of the word.

		/id/	/t/	/d/
1.	turned	☐	☐	☑
2.		☐	☐	☐
3.		☐	☐	☐
4.		☐	☐	☐
5.		☐	☐	☐
6.		☐	☐	☐
7.		☐	☐	☐
8.		☐	☐	☐
9.		☐	☐	☐
10.		☐	☐	☐

10 **Pronouncing -ed Endings** Work with a partner. Ask and answer the following questions in complete sentences. Pay attention to the pronunciation of the -ed endings.

1. When did you <u>move</u> to the place where you live now?
2. Who <u>decorated</u> your home?
3. When you were a child, how often did you <u>clean</u> your room?
4. When was the last time you <u>called</u> your family?
5. On your last vacation, who or what did you <u>miss</u> from home?

11 **Using -ed Endings** Look at the pictures. With a partner, talk about Olivia's moving day. Use the past tense of each verb. Pronounce the -ed endings carefully.

Example

Olivia and her roommate moved into her new place. First, the movers carri**ed** the boxes inside and Olivia watch**ed** them. Then, Olivia...

1.

move/carry/watch

2.

call/ask/describe

3.

look/decide

4.

unpack

5.

wash/drop

6.

dust/sneeze

7.

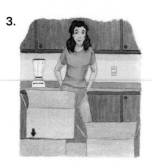

paint

8.

work/plant

9.

order

10.

rest

Talk It Over

12 Asking for Information About Housing Ads

1. Look at the three housing ads on page 91. What information is missing?
2. Ask five questions about the house or apartment in each ad. Use the ideas on the right.
3. Work with a partner. One of you is the manager, and the other is the renter. Create a dialogue using the questions you prepared.
4. Change roles for each ad.

1.

Huge apartment, sleeps four. Walk to campus. Call 510-555-2009 for more information.

Rent? _____

_____

Number of rooms? _____

_____

Noise? _____

_____

Stove/refrigerator? _____

_____

(Your own question) _____

_____

2.

2 bdr 2 bth $1,500 incl. utilities. No pets.Call for appointment 510-555-1828

Area? _____

_____

Lease? _____

_____

Garage? _____

_____

Number of bathrooms? _____

_____

(Your own question) _____

_____

3.

Roommate needed to share house. Private bth, share kitchen. No smokers, please.

Male/female? _____

_____

Number of rooms? _____

_____

Smoking? _____

_____

Location? _____

_____

Rent? _____

_____

Student Housing Choices

Before You Listen

1 **Prelistening Questions** You will hear a university advisor talk to students about housing. Before you listen, answer these questions with a partner.

1. What are some advantages (good things) and disadvantages (bad things) about the home you are living in now?

2. In your country, what housing choices do university students have?

3. Which kind of student living situation do you think you would like best? Why?

4. What can university students do to lower the cost of their living situation?

▲ A dorm room on a U.S. college campus

▲ Doing chores in a shared house

2 **Previewing Vocabulary** Listen to the underlined words from the presentation. Then write the letter of the correct definition for each underlined word beside each sentence.

Sentences

1. _____ My sister wants to build a <u>wing</u> on her home with an extra bedroom and bathroom for her growing family.

2. _____ Students in a dormitory don't have much <u>privacy</u> since several students share one room and one bathroom.

3. _____ The <u>hallways</u> in my dorm are so long – I have to walk by ten doors before I get to my room.

4. _____ Older hotels should be <u>updated</u> often if they want to look as good as brand new hotels.

5. _____ Rooms with private baths are more expensive than those with <u>common</u> bathrooms.

Definitions

a. a passageway or corridor

b. shared by two or more people

c. being separate or apart or, free from disturbance by others

d. a separate but connected area of a building

e. made more modern, with new furniture and new equipment

3 Listening for Main Ideas Listen to a college counselor give housing information to future students. To help you focus on some main points, take notes on these questions while you listen.

1. What are the two housing choices the advisor discusses?

2. Does the speaker directly say which housing choice is better?

3. Are the housing choices in the same location? Where is each one?

4 Taking Notes on Specific Information Listen again. Take notes about the advantages (pros) and disadvantages (cons) of each housing choice. Compare your list by speaking with a partner.

Housing Choice	Pros (good points)	Cons (bad points)
dorms	close to classes	

After You Listen

5 Summarizing Ideas Together with your partner, use notes from Activities 3 and 4 to compare the housing choices you heard about.

6 Using Vocabulary Discuss the following questions with a partner. Use the underlined vocabulary in your answers.

1. If you could build a new <u>wing</u> on your family home, what would you build?

2. How many emergency exits are there in your apartment building's (or school's) <u>hallway</u>?

3. How much <u>privacy</u> do you have in your present home? Is it enough or would you like more? Why?

4. Does anything in your family home need to be <u>updated</u>?

5. Do you and your parents or roommates share a <u>common</u> bathroom, or other common rooms?

Using Language Functions

Making and Answering Requests

It is important to learn how to make and answer formal and informal requests correctly.

	Making Requests	Answering Requests	
		Yes	**Formal**
Formal ↓ **Informal** **(or** **stronger)**	Could you...? Would you please...? Can you please...? Would you mind* _____ ing...? I'd like you to... I need you to... I want you to...	Certainly. Of course. I would be happy to. I don't mind.* Sure. Okay. No problem.	I'm afraid I can't I'm sorry, I can't. I'm sorry, but that's impossible. Absolutely not.** No way.**

*"Would you mind...?" means "Is it a problem for you?" The answer is negative:
"I don't mind" means "It's not a problem."

**"Absolutely not" and "No way" are strong refusals which could be considered rude.

---

7 **Role-Play** Work in pairs. Student A just moved into an off-campus apartment that needs many improvements. Student B is the manager of the apartment building. Student A asks Student B about the things that need to be fixed or changed. You may add your own ideas.

Problems

- the bedroom window is cracked
- the air conditioning is broken
- the fridge doesn't keep ice frozen
- there is only one electric plug in the kitchen
- you want a cat as a pet
- the bathroom walls are dark, old, and ugly
- (add 2–3 of your own ideas)

1. With your partner, role-play a conversation between the student and the manager. Use the expressions from the Making and Answering Requests chart above.

2. Switch roles and try the role-play again. Your teacher may ask you to share your role play with the class.

Talk about how the levels of politeness that each role-play used possibly affected the results.

Getting Meaning from Context

FOCUS ON TESTING

TOEFL® iBT

Using Context Clues

Many tests such as the TOEFL® iBT measure your academic listening and speaking abilities. This activity, and others in the book, will develop your social and academic communication abilities, and provide a foundation for success on a variety of standardized tests. Listen to the following conversations between roommates.

1. Listen to the beginning of each conversation.
2. Listen to the question for each conversation. Stop the recording and choose the best answer to each question. Remember to use clues, signals, words you know, grammar, stress, and intonation to help you guess.
3. In the **Clues** column, write the words that helped you choose your answer.
4. Listen to the last part of each conversation to hear the correct answer.

Answers	Clues
1. (A) the windows (B) the air conditioning (C) the heater	
2. (A) The woman lives alone. (B) The woman will break her lease. (C) The woman just moved.	
3. (A) two neighbors (B) renter and manager (C) roommates	
4. (A) The woman likes a different kind of music. (B) The neighbor's music is too loud. (C) The man has too many parties.	
5. (A) dormitory (B) private apartment (C) shared house	

Home Exchange: Taking Care of Someone's House

1 **Arranging a "Home Exchange"** When going on vacation, some people exchange homes rather than stay in hotels. Each home usually has some rules and responsibilities for the visitors.

1. Look at the rules and responsibilities in the charts below and on the next page. If you exchanged your home for a month, what rules would you give your guests? Discuss the possibilities with a partner or a small group.

2. Mary and Dave are old college friends – she lives in Los Angeles and he lives in New York. They are both in L.A. at Mary's, where Dave will stay for a month, but Mary will fly to N.Y. tonight and stay in Dave's home this month. Listen to their conversation, and complete the chart about things to do in each home.

▲ Mary's home in Los Angeles

▲ Dave's home in New York

Mary's Home

Rules
1. *don't* _____
2.
3.
4.
5.

Responsibilites

You need to...	Specific details or notes to remember
1. *water plants*	*1–2 times a week*
2.	
3.	
4.	

Dave's Apartment

Rules

1.
2.
3.

Responsibilites

You need to...	Specific details or notes to remember
1.	
2.	
3.	
4.	

2 **Listening to Instructions on Where to Put Furniture** Look at
Frederick's living room on page 98. His friend, Cynthia is a designer who is going to
suggest where he should put his new furniture.

1. Before you listen, look at the room and guess where the furniture should be.

2. Now listen to the designer's advice and write the name of each object in the
correct place on the picture.

▲ Frederick's living room

▲ easy chair

▲ sofa

▲ end table

▲ floor lamp

▲ coffee table

▲ television (TV)

3 **Comparing Pictures** Work in pairs. Student A should look at the picture on page 201. Student B should look at the picture on page 205. Tell each other about each item and its location in the room. Find ten differences without looking at each other's picture.

Example

A: In my picture, the closet door is open. There is a basketball on the floor.

B: In mine, the closet door is closed. The basketball was put away.

Self-Assessment Log

Check (✓) the words you learned in this chapter.

Nouns
- bus line
- hallways
- landlord
- laundry
- privacy
- security deposit
- unit
- wing

Verb
- require

Adjectives
- available
- common
- on-site
- refundable
- unfurnished
- updated

Check (✓) the things you did in this chapter. How well can you do each one?

	Very well	Fairly well	Not very well
I can listen to and practice stress and reductions.	☐	☐	☐
I can listen to and pronunce *-ed* endings	☐	☐	☐
I can understand and talk about housing ads.	☐	☐	☐
I can make and answer requests.	☐	☐	☐
I can guess meanings from context.	☐	☐	☐
I can talk about home exchanges and home care.	☐	☐	☐

Write what you learned and liked in this chapter.

In this chapter,

I learned _____

_____

I liked _____

_____

6 Cultures of the World

> "No culture has a monopoly on beauty and no religion has a monopoly on truth."
>
> Voltaire (François-Marie Arouet)
> French writer and philosopher

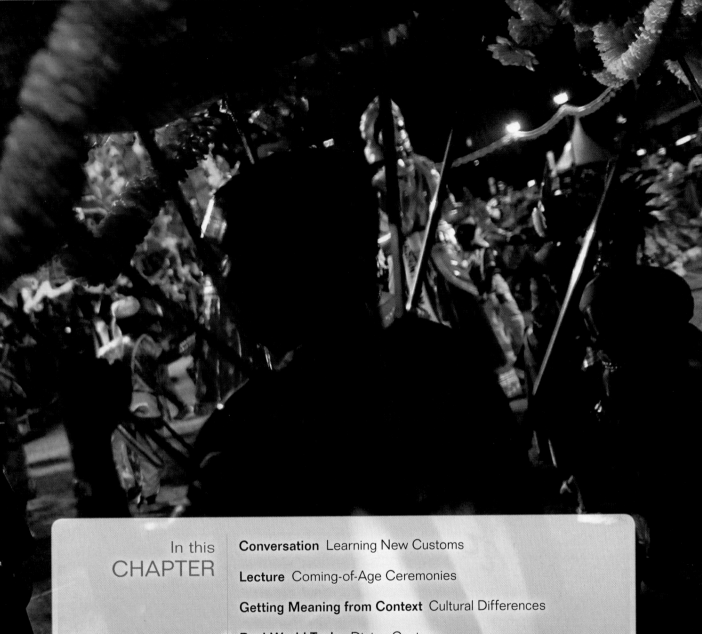

In this
CHAPTER

Conversation Learning New Customs

Lecture Coming-of-Age Ceremonies

Getting Meaning from Context Cultural Differences

Real-World Tasks Dining Customs

Connecting to the Topic

1 Look at the photo. How are these people celebrating?

2 What kind of celebration do you think this is? Name five other kinds of celebrations.

3 What places and cultures are you interested in? Why?

Learning New Customs

Before You Listen

1 **Prelistening Questions** Before you listen, talk about travel with a partner.

▲ Salma talking on her cell phone.

1. Discuss the situation in the photo. Why shouldn't Salma use her cell phone?

2. Do you know the expression "When in Rome, do as the Romans do"? Talk about a time when you followed this advice.

3. How do you feel when you travel to a new place, meet new people, and experience new customs? Circle the words in the box that describe how you feel. Explain or give examples of times that you have had these feelings.

afraid	curious	excited	interested	shy
careful	energetic	homesick	nervous	worried

2 **Previewing Vocabulary** Listen to the underlined words. You will hear these words in the conversation. Then use the context to guess their meanings. Write your guesses in the spaces.

Contexts	Meanings
1. My first <u>impression</u> of my new boss was not good. He seemed strict and unfriendly when I first met him, but now I like him.	
2. I don't like getting up at 6 A.M., but I am <u>used to</u> it now because I've been doing it every day for three years.	
3. Mr. and Mrs. Haley like to travel to <u>exotic</u> places. They like unusual and interesting vacations.	
4. If you don't finish your food in an American restaurant, you can take the remaining food home in a <u>doggie bag</u>.	
5. When I arrived in the U.S., I was <u>amazed</u> by the number of large cars on the road. There were so many! We have only small cars where I'm from.	
6. Our teacher has not given us a lot of homework <u>so far</u>, but maybe she'll give us more next week.	
7. When we finished dinner, we put the <u>leftovers</u> in the refrigerator.	

Listen

3 **Listening for Main Ideas** Kenji is having lunch with Yolanda and her friend Salma, who is visiting from Lebanon. Close your book and listen to the conversation. Listen for the answers to these questions.

1. What is Salma's impression of the United States?
2. What surprised Salma in the restaurant?

Compare and discuss your answers with a partner.

4 **Listening for Details** Listen to the conversation again if necessary. Write *T* if a statement is true and *F* if it is false.

1. _____ Salma doesn't like hot dogs because they don't taste good.

2. _____ Kenji likes American food.

3. _____ At the Mexican restaurant, Yolanda was surprised when Salma asked for a doggie bag.

4. _____ In Salma's country, using cell phones is common everywhere.

5. _____ Salma says "When in Rome, do as the Romans do" to mean that she will start eating American food.

Stress

5 **Listening for Stressed Words** Listen to part of the conversation again. Some of the stressed words are missing. During each pause, repeat the phrase or sentence. Then fill in the blanks with the words you hear.

Kenji: So, Salma, is this your _____ trip to the United States?

Salma: Yes, it is.

Kenji: And what's your _____ so far?

Salma: Well, the people are really _____, and the city is beautiful. But the _____; well, it's not so good.

Kenji: Oh, yeah, that's what I thought too when I _____ got here. But I'm _____ to American food now. I actually _____ hot dogs and French fries.

Yolanda: So last night I took Salma to a _____ restaurant. I wanted her to try something _____.

Kenji: Did you _____ it?

Salma: Yeah, the food was _____ good, but it was _____ _____. I couldn't _____ it all.

Yolanda: Salma was _____ when I took the _____ home in a doggie bag.

Kenji: Yeah, that's funny, _____ it? They call it a _____ bag, but it's for people. Anyway, what _____ surprised you?

Salma: That the restaurant was so _____! We don't use

_____ conditioning so much in my country. Oh, and the

water had _____ in it, too. I had to put on my

_____, I was so cold!

Now read the conversation with two other classmates. Practice stressing words correctly.

Reductions

6 **Comparing Unreduced and Reduced Pronunciation** The following sentences come from the conversation. Listen for the difference between unreduced and reduced pronunciation. Repeat both forms after the speaker.

Unreduced Pronunciation	**Reduced Pronunciation***
1. Is this your first trip to the United States?	Is thishyer first trip to the United States?
2. What's your impression so far?	Whatcher impression so far?
3. I wanted her to try something exotic.	I wanted 'er ta try something exotic.

* Note: The underlined forms are not acceptable spellings in written English.

7 **Listening for Reductions** Anita and Brenda have just finished eating lunch together. Listen to their conversation. Repeat each sentence during the pause. Then write the unreduced forms of the missing words in the blanks.

Anita: Well, it's time to get back to the office. I'll see you soon, Brenda.

Brenda: OK, see you… Wait, Anita, is _____ _____

cell phone?

Anita: Oh my goodness, yes, thanks. By the way, I almost forgot: my

parents are coming _____ a visit next week.

Brenda: Really? I'd love _____ meet _____.

Anita: Well, _____ _____ _____

_____ have lunch with us on Saturday?

Brenda: Saturday? Hmm… I promised my roommate I would go shopping

with _____ that day. Could we get together

_____ coffee later in the afternoon?

Anita: I _____ _____. They might be busy, but I'll ask.

With a partner, read the conversation. Practice reduced pronunciation.

8 Using Vocabulary Discuss the following questions with a partner. Use the underlined vocabulary in your answers.

1. Do you remember the first time you visited a foreign country? What was your first <u>impression</u> of it?

2. Has anything changed in your life in the past year? For example, did you start a new job? Did you move to a new place? Are you <u>used to</u> the new situation in your life?

3. What is the most <u>exotic</u> place or food that you have experienced in your life?

4. What would happen if an American asked for a <u>doggie bag</u> in your country?

5. How many years of education have you completed <u>so far</u>?

6. What <u>amazes</u> you about the United States or another country you have visited? Finish this sentence: "I am <u>amazed</u> that...."

7. Some people hate to eat <u>leftovers</u>. How about you?

Talk It Over

9 Discussing Behavior In this section you learned the expression "When in Rome, do as the Romans do." But is this always a good rule to follow? Work in small groups and discuss the following questions.

1. Have you ever been in a situation where everyone was behaving in a way that you didn't like? How did you feel? What did you do?

2. In what situations might it be impossible for you to "do as the Romans do"? Brainstorm a list of situations. What would you do if you found yourself in one of these situations?

▲ Would you talk on your cell phone in a quiet place? Would you ask someone to stop talking on their cell phone in a quiet place?

Coming-of-Age Ceremonies

Before You Listen

1 **Prelistening Questions** Before you listen, talk with a partner about coming of age in different countries.

1. At what age does a person come of age, or become a legal adult, in your culture?

2. Do you know of any special customs or ceremonies when a person becomes an adult? Is it different for boys and girls?

▲ These young women celebrate Coming-of-Age Day in Japan.

2 **Previewing Vocabulary** You will hear the following words in the lecture. Listen to the words. Then write the letter of the correct definition beside each word.

Words

1. _____ the woods
2. _____ adult
3. _____ adulthood
4. _____ ceremony
5. _____ responsible for (something)
6. _____ passage
7. _____ look forward to (something)

Definitions

a. a formal or traditional way of celebrating an important event

b. the time of life when a person is not a child anymore

c. to wait for an event with a feeling of excitement

d. a movement to the next stage or level of something

e. an area thickly covered with trees

f. in control of something and taking care of it

g. a person who is grown up, not a child anymore

Listen

3 **Listening for Main Ideas** Listen to a short lecture about becoming an adult in four different cultures. As you listen, list the cultures in the spaces below.

Culture 1

Culture 2

Culture 3

Culture 4

4 Taking Notes on Specific Information Listen again. This time, fill in the details about each culture or religion.

Culture / Religion	Age	Details
1. North American Indian	12–13	
2.		
3.		
4.		

After You Listen

 5 Summarizing Ideas In groups of four, use your notes from Activities 3 and 4 to summarize the lecture. Each student should speak about one culture. Try to speak in complete sentences.

 6 Using Vocabulary Discuss the following questions with a partner. Use the underlined vocabulary in your answers.

1. Are you legally an <u>adult</u> in your country? What about in the United States?
2. Which is easier, in your opinion: <u>adulthood</u> or childhood? Why?
3. In your community, is there a <u>ceremony</u> when a baby is born? If yes, describe it.
4. When you were a teenager, were you <u>responsible for</u> watching your younger brothers and sisters? How did you feel about this responsibility?

5. What has been the most important <u>passage</u> in your life until now?

6. Are you <u>looking forward to</u> the next passage in your life (graduation, marriage, children, retirement, etc.)? Why or why not?

7. How would you feel about going into <u>the woods</u> alone for three days? Why would you feel this way?

Talk It Over

7 **At What Age...?** Work in small groups. Talk about when people should be allowed to do the following activities.

Example

I think 16 is too young to get a driver's license. Age 18 is better because...

▲ A teenage driver

Activity	Age
get a driver's license	
get married with parents' permission	
get married without parents' permission	
vote	
get a credit card	
live away from parents	
join the army	
become president of your country	
retire (with full government benefits)	

Getting Meaning from Context

Strategy

Graphic Organizer: Matrix Diagram
A matrix diagram organizes information about two or more characteristics of two or more topics. You can use a matrix diagram to:
- show the characteristics clearly
- study and remember the characteristics
- compare the characteristics
- organize your ideas about the characteristics

1 Prelistening Discussion When you visit other countries, it's important to know the local customs. Polite behavior in one culture can be rude in another culture. For example, kissing a friend to say hello is common in France but not in Korea. Give examples of some polite and rude behaviors from your culture. Discuss with your group and fill in the chart.

Polite Behaviors	Rude Behaviors
being on time for appointments	being late for an appointment and not calling

FOCUS ON TESTING

TOEFL® iBT

Using Context Clues

Many tests such as the TOEFL® iBT measure your academic listening and speaking abilities. This activity, and others in the book, will develop your social and academic communication abilities, and provide a foundation for success on a variety of standardized tests. The following five conversations take place in North America. In each situation, one speaker's action is "culturally incorrect." Listen and decide what the mistake is.

1. Listen to the beginning of each conversation.

2. Listen to the question for each conversation. Stop the recording and choose the best answer to each question.

3. In the **Clues** column, write the words that helped you choose your answer.

4. Start the recording again. Listen to the last part of each conversation to hear the correct answer.

Answers	Clues
1. (A) She didn't call before visiting. (B) She didn't bring a present. (C) She used Belinda's first name.	
2. (A) He didn't eat all his food. (B) He forgot to leave a tip. (C) He asked for the check.	
3. (A) The guests did because they were late. (B) The neighbor did because she wasn't ready. (C) The man did because he came too early.	
4. (A) He asked about the price of the house. (B) He asked too many questions. (C) He asked the woman for a drink.	
5. (A) that Koreans hug people on their birthdays (B) that Koreans don't celebrate birthdays (C) that Koreans don't hug people they don't know very well	

2 Comparing Customs Review the social mistakes you heard in the Focus on Testing activity. With a partner, make a statement about each custom. Then compare it to customs in other countries.

1. In American restaurants, a 15 to 20 percent tip is normal. But in _____

   _____

2. Before visiting someone in the United States, it's better to call first. But in

   _____

3. _____

   _____

4. _____

   _____

5. _____

   _____

Using Language Functions

FOCUS

Apologizing

The following expressions are often used after we make a mistake and feel bad about a situation. The mistake may be small (stepping on someone's foot) or serious (being a half hour late for a test).

	Apologizing	Responding
Informal	Oops! Excuse me.	Forget about it.
	Sorry.	Don't worry about it.
	I'm (very) sorry.	No problem.
	It was my fault.	That's okay.
	I apologize.	That's all right.
Formal	Please forgive me.	I forgive you.

3 **Role-Play** Read the following situations. With a partner, prepare a conversation about each situation. Use the appropriate expressions for apologizing and responding.

▲ It's 6 o'clock in the morning on a Saturday.

Situations

1. It's 6 o'clock in the morning on a Saturday. Your neighbor comes to your door to complain that your music is too loud.

2. You forgot about your doctor's appointment at 3:00 P.M. today. The doctor's secretary calls you to ask what happened.

3. You don't feel well and you need to leave in the middle of the class.

4. You see an old friend and she looks like she has gained weight. You think she is pregnant. You ask her when the baby is due. She says she is not pregnant.

Dining Customs

Culture Note

Formal Dining

Family dinners in the United States are usually relaxed and informal. However, sometimes, when special guests are invited, or if you are eating in a restaurant, dinners are more formal and traditional.

A formal American dinner usually has the following parts, served in order:

1. soup
2. salad
3. the *main course* (meat, chicken, or fish; potato or rice; and one or more cooked vegetables)
4. dessert (something sweet such as cake, ice cream, or fruit)

Typically, bread and butter are served before the salad is served. Water is almost always served.

While you are waiting for your meal, sometimes an appetizer (a small dish) will be served.

▲ A formal dinner party in the United States.

1 Prelistening Questions Before you listen, talk about dining customs with a partner.

1. What are the typical parts of a formal dinner in your culture?

2. What special foods or drinks are served at formal dinners that you don't usually have every day?

3. Have you ever eaten in a formal restaurant or at a formal dinner party? Describe this experience.

2 Previewing Vocabulary Listen to the underlined words. You will hear these words in the conversation. Before you listen, use the context to guess their definitions. Write the letter of the correct definition beside each sentence.

Sentences

1. _____ Take a couple of <u>napkins</u>. These sandwiches are really messy.

2. _____ When I was a teenager, it was my job to <u>set the table</u> each night before dinner.

3. _____ In a restaurant, it is a waiter's job to <u>serve</u> the food and drinks.

4. _____ Please <u>lay</u> that box on the dining room table.

5. _____ Most Europeans use <u>silverware</u> to eat with, while many Asians prefer chopsticks.

6. _____ Be careful with that knife! Pick it up only by the <u>handle</u>.

7. _____ A: What kind of kitchen <u>utensil</u> is this?
   B: It's a potato peeler. It's much easier to use than a knife.

8. _____ It is <u>logical</u> not to eat food that tastes bad.

Definitions

a. any kind of kitchen tool

b. knives, forks, and spoons

c. the part of a tool that you hold in your hand

d. to put dishes, plates, glasses, etc. on a table before a meal

e. reasonable or sensible

f. put something down

g. to give or bring something to a customer

h. a piece of cloth or paper used to protect your clothes and wipe your mouth while eating

3 Following Directions for Setting a Table Ming loves cooking and entertaining. For Peter's 23rd birthday, she wants to prepare a formal dinner for their friends. She asks Peter's mother, Mrs. Riley, to teach her how to set a formal dinner table.

Listen to the conversation between Ming and Mrs. Riley. Follow Mrs. Riley's instructions for setting the table. As she mentions each item, write its number in the proper place.

1. dinner napkin
2. water glass
3. white wine glass
4. red wine glass
5. bread plate
6. soup spoon
7. coffee spoon
8. dinner fork
9. salad fork
10. dessert fork
11. butter knife
12. dinner knife

4 **Using Vocabulary** With a partner, look at the picture from Activity 3. Take turns naming the numbered items and saying where they belong. Begin like this: "Number 1 is a napkin. It goes on the dinner plate." Then answer the questions below.

1. In your family, who serves the food when you eat together? Who sets the table?

2. What is your favorite or most useful kitchen utensil?

3. When you come home from school, where do you lay your books?

4. Do you think it is more logical to eat dessert before or after a meal? Why?

5. Name several utensils that have handles.

5 **Talking About Table Manners** "Table manners" are polite behavior we use when eating. The picture below contains examples of behaviors that are rude in the United States. Work in small groups. Identify the rude behaviors. Write your answers on a separate piece of paper. Then discuss the questions on the next page.

1. Which of these behaviors would be bad manners in other cultures?

2. Which would not? What are some other eating behaviors that are rude in other cultures?

Self-Assessment Log

Check (✓) the words you learned in this chapter.

Nouns		Verbs	Adjectives
▦ adult	▦ passage	▦ lay	▦ amazed
▦ adulthood	▦ silverware	▦ look forward to	▦ exotic
▦ ceremony	▦ utensil	(something)	▦ logical
▦ doggie bag	▦ the woods	▦ serve	▦ responsible for
▦ handle		▦ set the table	(something)
▦ impression			
▦ leftovers			**Expressions**
▦ napkin			▦ so far
			▦ used to

Check (✓) the things you did in this chapter. How well can you do each one?

	Very well	Fairly well	Not very well
I can listen to and practice stress and reductions.	☐	☐	☐
I can talk about cultural differences.	☐	☐	☐
I can take notes on a lecture.	☐	☐	☐
I can summarize my notes.	☐	☐	☐
I can guess meanings from context.	☐	☐	☐
I can make and respond to apologies.	☐	☐	☐
I can talk about dining customs and table manners.	☐	☐	☐

Write what you learned and liked in this chapter.

In this chapter,

I learned _____

_____

I liked _____

_____

7 Health

"Laughter is the best medicine."

Proverb

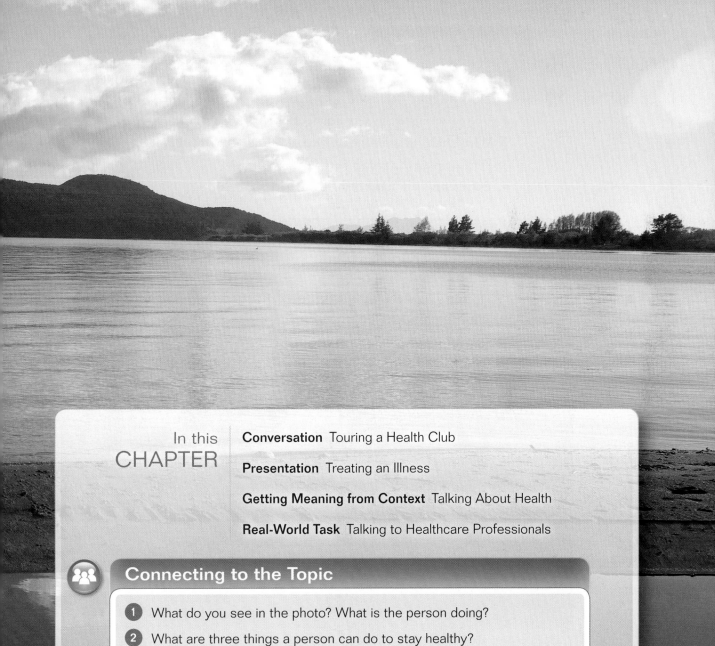

In this
CHAPTER

Conversation Touring a Health Club

Presentation Treating an Illness

Getting Meaning from Context Talking About Health

Real-World Task Talking to Healthcare Professionals

Connecting to the Topic

1. What do you see in the photo? What is the person doing?

2. What are three things a person can do to stay healthy?

3. What are the most popular forms of exercise in your country? Why do you think they are so popular?

Touring a Health Club

Before You Listen

1 **Prelistening Questions** Before you listen, talk about your health with a partner.

1. Do you belong to a gym or health club? How often do you go?
2. What kinds of classes and activities do health clubs offer?
3. What activities do you do to try to stay healthy?
4. Do you have any habits that are bad for your health?

▲ Kenji and Peter tour a health club.

2 **Previewing Vocabulary** Listen to these words and phrases from the conversation. Then complete the sentences with the words and phrases.

Nouns		Verbs	Expression
boxing	lane	jog	in good/bad shape
cardio	locker room	lift weights	
discount	yoga	ought to	
health club		show (someone) around	
		swim	

1. The new _____ will be very popular because it has a huge swimming pool, a great weight room, lots of exercise equipment, and a cool juice bar.

2. Some people _____ at health clubs to build stronger and bigger muscles.

3. Judy goes to the gym three times a week because she wants to be _____. She likes to look and feel healthy.

4. The swimming pool at my gym is separated into three sections. Fast swimmers swim in the middle _____ and slow swimmers swim in the other two.

5. Right now there is a 15 percent _____ on all running shoes. I got a $100.00 pair of shoes for $85.00.

6. If you want to take a _____ class, you need to buy special gloves and shoes. You need something to protect your teeth, too, in case you get hit in the mouth.

7. She likes to _____ five miles every morning before breakfast. She has to buy new running shoes every six months.

8. If you want to lose weight, you _____ eat less and exercise more.

9. If you'd like to see all of the different rooms that our health club has, I can _____ you _____.

10. _____ helps me to relax and stretch my muscles.

11. I love my _____ class because our teacher always chooses great, fast music for exercising. The music is so energizing that it's easy to jump around for an hour.

12. You can leave your clothes in the _____ when you go out to _____ in the pool.

3 **Listening for Main Ideas** Peter and Kenji want to get in shape. Close your book and listen to the conversation. Listen for the answers to these questions.

1. Where are Peter and Kenji? Do you think they like this place? How do you know?

2. What is the purpose of the tour? What would the guide like Peter and Kenji to do?

Compare and discuss your answers with a partner.

4 **Listening for Details** Listen again if necessary. Answer the questions.

1. What kind of exercise class did Peter and Kenji see?

2. What other classes does this gym offer?

3. Who was the fast swimmer in the pool?

4. Why should Peter and Kenji join the club this month?

Stress

5 **Listening for Stressed Words** Listen to the conversation again. Some of the stressed words are missing. During each pause, repeat the phrase or sentence. Then fill in the blanks with the words you hear.

Adel: Hi, I'm Adel. I'm _____ you're going to _____ it here. Let me show you _____. Here's the _____ room. We've got the newest machines, and our instructors can _____ you how to _____ them.

Peter: This is _____!

Kenji: Yeah. I really need to start _____ _____.

Adel: And here is a _____ class...

Peter: I've _____ tried cardio. It's just _____, isn't it?

Adel: Not really. Actually, they're working _____ than you _____.

Kenji: And cardio is very good for your _____.

Adel: It sure is. But you should do it at least _____ times a week if you want to be in _____ _____.

Peter: Well, I already _____ three times a week.

Adel: That's _____.

Kenji: You also have _____ and _____ classes here, _____ you?

Adel: Yes. I'll give you a _____ of classes when we finish our _____. Now here's our _____ pool.

Peter: Wow! Look at that woman in the _____ lane. She's really fast, _____ she!

Adel: Oh, yeah. That's Ellen, one of our _____.

Kenji: _____ like to take lessons from _____!

Adel: You're not the _____ one. C'mon, I'll show you the _____ and the locker room.

You know, if you want to _____ our gym, you _____ to do it _____ the end of the month.

Kenji: Really? Why?

Adel: Well, because we have a special _____ for students this month. _____ go to my office and I'll _____ you all about it.

Now read the conversation with two other classmates. Practice stressing words correctly.

After You Listen

6 Using Vocabulary Discuss the following questions with a partner. Use the underlined vocabulary in your answers.

1. Which of the following activities have you tried? Did you like or dislike them? Why?

   lifting weights   jogging   boxing   yoga   swimming

2. Are you in good shape now? If yes, how do you keep in shape? If not, what can you do to get in shape?

3. Are you a good swimmer? When did you learn to swim? How did you learn? If you can't swim, are you interested in learning? Why or why not?

4. Do you think it's fair that students and senior citizens can get discounts at health clubs, theaters, restaurants, and other places? Why or why not?

5. Is it safe to leave your money and other valuable things in the locker room at a gym? Why or why not?

6. Your friend wants to get in shape quickly. Tell your friend what he or she ought to do.

Pronunciation

Intonation with Tag Questions

A tag question is a statement with a "tag" at the end. Affirmative statements take negative tags, and negative statements take affirmative tags.

For example:

He's strong, isn't he?   You're not tired, are you?

People pronounce tag questions in two ways. Listen to the following examples. Notice the difference in intonation.

<table>
<tr><th>Rising Intonation</th><th>Falling Intonation</th></tr>
</table>

Your father is a doctor, isn't he?   Your father is a doctor, isn't he?

In the first example, the speaker isn't sure of the answer. He is asking for information, so his voice goes up at the end of the sentence:

Your father is a doctor, isn't he?

In the second example, the speaker is sure that the father is a doctor. The question is not a real question; instead, it is a way of "making conversation." The speaker's voice goes down at the end of the sentence:

Your father is a doctor, isn't he?

7 **Pronouncing Tag Questions** Listen and repeat the sentences. The first five are asking for information, so they have rising intonation. The second five are ways of making conversation. They have falling intonation.

1. We need special shoes for cardio, don't we?
2. The pool is warm, isn't it?
3. You play football, don't you?
4. You don't eat junk food, do you?
5. You didn't hurt yourself, did you?
6. My father looks healthy, doesn't he?
7. This exercise is hard, isn't it?
8. Your parents love to dance, don't they?
9. She can swim fast, can't she?
10. It's a beautiful day, isn't it?

8 Understanding Tag Questions Listen to tag questions from the dialogue. From the intonation, decide if the speaker is asking a real question or just "making conversation." Circle the correct answer.

1. Asking a question   Making conversation

2. Asking a question   Making conversation

3. Asking a question   Making conversation

4. Asking a question   Making conversation

5. Asking a question   Making conversation

6. Asking a question   Making conversation

Using Language Functions

FOCUS

Forming Tag Questions

When the verb *be* is used in the main statement of the sentence, use *be* to form the tag question. For example:

Vic **is** tired, **isn't** he?   Lori **isn't** here, **is** she?

When a modal verb (like *can, could, should, would*) is used in the main statement of the sentence, use the same verb to form the tag question. For example:

Tzu Han **can** swim, **can't** she?   Yong Jin **shouldn't** go, **should** he?

When other verbs are used in the main statement of the sentence, use *do* to form the tag question. For example:

Farida **plays** tennis, **doesn't** she?   Linda **doesn't** have a car, **does** she?

9 Using Tag Questions Work with a partner. Each of you will look at a different set of sentences in the box on page 128. Add a tag question to each sentence. Use rising intonation if you don't know what your partner's answer will be. Use falling intonation if you know the answer. You should both answer truthfully.*

Example

(Hamburgers are fattening.)

Student A asks: Hamburgers are fattening, aren't they?

Student B answers: Yes, I think so. (means Student A is correct.)

* If a tag question is affirmative, answer "No" if you agree with the speaker. Answer "Yes" if you
disagree. For example:
A: There's no homework tonight, is there?
B: No, there isn't. (means Speaker A is correct) OR
B: Yes, there is. (means Speaker A is incorrect)

Student A

1. You're from _____ (name of city), _____?

2. The weather is _____ today, _____?

3. There's no homework tonight, _____?

4. You play tennis, _____?

5. Jogging is very boring, _____?

Student B

1. You have a (large/small) family, _____?

2. This classroom is very _____, _____?

3. Milk isn't healthy for adults, _____?

4. This lesson is _____, _____?

5. American health clubs are expensive, _____?

Talk It Over

10 Talking About Stress You are going to complete a questionnaire about stress. First, discuss the following questions with your classmates and your teacher.

1. What is stress?

2. What causes stress?

3. What can be the results of living with too much stress?

4. When do you feel you are under a lot of stress?

▲ A woman meditating in nature

▲ Analysts worried about the financial crisis

11 Completing a Questionnaire About Stress Complete the following questionnaire.*

How stressful is your life? Give yourself points from one to five on each item:

1 = almost always

2 = often

3 = sometimes

4 = seldom

5 = never

1. _____ I eat at least one hot, nutritious meal a day (a meal that has all the basic foods needed for good health).

2. _____ I get seven to eight hours of sleep at least four nights a week.

3. _____ I give and receive affection regularly.

4. _____ I have at least one relative within fifty miles on whom I can rely, who could help me if I needed help.

5. _____ I exercise fairly heavily (to the point of perspiration) at least twice a week.

6. _____ I am the appropriate weight for my height.

7. _____ I have an income that is enough to meet the basic expenses.

8. _____ I get strength from my religious beliefs.

9. _____ I regularly attend club or social activities.

10. _____ I have a network, or group, of friends and acquaintances.

11. _____ I have one or more friends to talk to about personal matters.

12. _____ I am in good health (including eyesight, hearing, teeth).

13. _____ I am able to speak openly about my feelings when angry or worried.

14. _____ I have regular conversations with the people I live with about domestic problems—for example, chores, money, and daily living issues.

15. _____ I do something for fun at least once a week.

16. _____ I am able to organize my time effectively.

17. _____ I drink fewer than three cups of coffee (or tea or cola drinks) a day.

18. _____ I take quiet time for myself during the day.

* Questionnaire and scoring chart taken from "How Vulnerable Are You to Stress?", *Time* magazine, © Time Inc. Reprinted by permission.

To find your score, add up the numbers and subtract 20. Then check the chart below to analyze your score.

	If your score is...	you are...
Safe Zone	below 25	living a calm, unstressful life.
Leaving the Safe Zone	between 25 and 45	living with more stress than experts consider healthy. Maybe you should think about making some changes.
Moving Near the Danger Zone	between 45 and 70	approaching the danger zone. Which of the 18 areas can you change?
Danger Zone	over 70	living with entirely too much stress. You may have serious problems as a result.

 12 Follow-Up Discuss these questions with the whole class or in small groups.

1. Who had the highest score in the class? The lowest?

2. Look at the 18 items. Find two areas that you would like to change in your life. Tell your classmates about these two areas. Then listen as they tell you about the areas they would like to change.

Treating an Illness

Before You Listen

 1 Prelistening Questions Before you listen, talk about the flu with a partner.

1. Have you ever had the flu (influenza)?

2. What are the *symptoms* of the flu? (For example: a fever)

3. Is the flu dangerous? Why or why not?

4. Imagine that you are a doctor. What advice would you give a patient who has the flu?

Strategy

Graphic Organizer: Problem-Solution Chart

You can use a problem-solution chart to list problems and possible ways to solve them. In the chart below, the problem column is Symptoms of the Flu and the solution column is Treatment of the Flu.

2 Previewing Vocabulary Listen to the words from the conversation. Then in a small group, divide the words and phrases into two groups in the graphic organizer below: "Symptoms of the Flu" and "Treatment of the Flu." Use a dictionary if necessary.

Culture Note

In many countries, including the United States you must get a **prescription** from a doctor in order to buy certain medicines. A **prescription** is an official piece of paper with the name of the medicine and other important information. You take the **prescription** to a pharmacy to get the medicine.

Nouns	Adjectives	Expression
aspirin	swollen	eat right
fever	weak	
headache		
prescription		
rest		
sore throat		
upset stomach		

Symptoms of the Flu	Treatment of the Flu

The following body parts are mentioned in the conversation. Write definitions for them before you listen. Work with a partner.

muscle _____

forehead _____

throat _____

3 **Listening for Main Ideas** Barbara is at the university health clinic. Listen to her conversation with her doctor. As you listen, answer these questions.

1. What is wrong with Barbara?
2. What does the doctor tell her to do?

4 **Taking Notes on Specific Information** Listen to the conversation again. This time, take notes in the problem-solution chart below.

Barbara's Complaints	Doctor's Advice
1.	
2.	
3.	
4.	
5.	
6.	

After You Listen

5 **Summarizing Ideas** Use past-tense verbs to summarize Barbara's visit to the doctor. Include her symptoms and the doctor's advice.

Example

Barbara went to the doctor because she woke up with a terrible headache. She told the doctor...

6 Reviewing Vocabulary Answer the questions with a classmate.

1. Look back at Activity 2 on page 131. Which symptoms did you have the last time you had the flu or a cold?

2. How often do you take pain relievers such as aspirin?

3. Look back at the doctor's advice. Which advice do you agree with, or disagree with? Why?

Using Language Functions

FOCUS

Giving Advice

Here are some expressions for asking for and giving advice.

Asking for Advice	Giving Advice
What do you think I should do? What do you think I ought to do? Should I _____? Can you give me some/any advice?	You should... You ought to... Try to... Why don't you... I advise you to...

▲ "Can you give me some advice?"

7 Asking for and Giving Advice

1. Work with a partner. Describe the problem in each of the following pictures.
2. Match the picture with the correct remedy (treatment).
3. Finally, role-play each situation. One person describes the problem and asks for advice. The other person gives advice.

Example

A: I have a headache. Should I go to a doctor?

B: I don't think so. Why don't you take an aspirin?

> **Possible Remedies**
>
> **a.** Drink tea.
> **b.** Take a cold shower.
> **c.** Bandage it.
> **d.** Put ice on it.
> **e.** Take a sleeping pill.

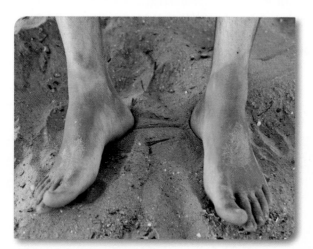

1. _____

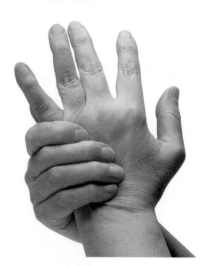

2. _____

3. _____

4. _____

5. _____

Getting Meaning from Context

FOCUS ON TESTING

TOEFL® iBT

Using Context Clues

Many tests such as the TOEFL® iBT measure your academic listening and speaking abilities. This activity, and others in the book, will develop your social and communication skills, and provide a foundation for success on a variety of standardized tests. Each of the following four conversations has one surprising or unusual thing in it.

1. Listen to each conversation. Then listen to the question. Stop the recording after the question, and write what is strange in the **Answers** column in the chart.

2. In the **Clues** column, write the words that helped you choose your answer.

3. Start the recording again.

4. Listen to the next part of the conversation to hear the correct answer.

Answers	Clues
1.	
2.	
3.	
4.	

Now listen to the following conversations. What are they about? Choose the best answer to each question.

1. Ⓐ Nancy's having an operation.
   Ⓑ Nancy's going to have a baby.
   Ⓒ Nancy's working at the hospital.

2. Ⓐ coffee shop
   Ⓑ supermarket
   Ⓒ health food store

1 **Role-Play** People have different ways of getting help with their personal problems. Some people visit psychologists for advice, while others talk to their close friends and family members about their problems.

Culture Note

A **psychologist** is an advisor or a counselor who helps people with their personal problems. People from some cultures may think only "crazy" people visit psychologists. However, in the United States and Canada, many people feel comfortable getting advice from professionals who are trained to help them.

With a partner, prepare a role-play taking the roles of a friend or family member and someone with one of the problems in the box below.

> You are very shy at parties and at work.
> You cannot stay with just one girlfriend/boyfriend.
> You are jealous of your very successful sister.
> You work 18 hours a day and don't know how to relax.

▲ Which woman is offering advice?

Talk It Over

2 Discussing Your Opinion In small groups, read the statements about smoking. Then say whether you agree or disagree with each statement. Give reasons for your opinion.

▲ You cannot smoke in this place. What kind of place do you think this is?

1. Smoking should be forbidden in:

   - restaurants
   - movie theaters
   - classrooms
   - bars
   - public transportation
   - hospitals
   - discos/nightclubs
   - (your suggestion): _____

2. It should be illegal to sell cigarettes to anyone under the age of 18.

3. If a smoker gets cancer, it's his own fault. Nobody forced him to smoke.

4. If a smoker gets cancer, the tobacco companies should pay her medical bills.

5. It is wrong to advertise cigarettes to teenagers.

6. I would not date a person who smokes.

7. Governments should educate their people, especially teenagers, about the dangers of smoking.

8. If parents smoke, their children will probably smoke also.

9. There should not be cigarette advertising:

   - on television
   - on the radio
   - in magazines
   - on billboards

Talking to Health Care Professionals

 1 **Taking Notes on Phone Conversations** You will hear three telephone conversations about health situations. Take notes on each call.

Conversation 1

Reason for call: _____

_____

Name of dentist: _____

Location: _____

Time of appointment: _____

Conversation 2

Reason for call: _____

_____

Name of patient: _____

Price of medicine: _____

Special instructions: _____

Closing time: _____

Conversation 3

First reason for call: _____

_____

Name of baby's doctor: _____

Time of baby's new appointment: _____

Second reason for call: _____

_____

Time of husband's appointment: _____

Name of husband's doctor: _____

2 **Making Appointments with Doctors** Choose one of the situations from this page or the next page to role-play with a partner. Look only at the box for your role. Do not look at your partner's information!

Situation 1: Dentist's office

Roles: patient and receptionist

Patient's Instructions

1. Call the dentist's office to change your appointment. Tell the receptionist:
   a. the time of your old appointment
   b. the reason for the change
2. Arrange a new appointment time with the receptionist.

Receptionist's Instructions

1. A patient will call you to change an appointment. Answer the phone politely; then listen to the patient's problem.
2. Arrange a new appointment time with the patient.

Situation 2: Doctor's office

Roles: patient and receptionist

Patient's Instructions

1. Call the doctor's office to make an appointment. Tell the receptionist:
   a. your medical problem (why you're calling)
   b. when you want to come in
2. Ask where you can park.

Receptionist's Instructions

1. A patient will call you to make an appointment. Answer the phone politely; then listen to the patient's problem.
2. Arrange an appointment time with the patient. Answer the patient's questions.

Situation 3: Doctor's office

Roles: patient and doctor

Patient's Instructions

1. You have a strange medical problem. Tell your doctor:
   a. your symptoms
   b. when they started
   c. how often you have them

Doctor's Instructions

1. Listen to a patient tell you about his or her strange symptoms.

2. Ask the patient when these symptoms started and how often they happen.

3. Tell the patient that he or she has an unusual disease and give the patient instructions about how to treat the problem.

"I'd like to change my appointment. Do ▶ you have anything available tomorrow?"

Self-Assessment Log

Check (✓) the words you learned in this chapter.

Nouns		Verbs	Adjectives
▨ aspirin	▨ locker room	▨ jog	▨ swollen
▨ boxing	▨ prescription	▨ lift weights	▨ weak
▨ cardio	▨ rest	▨ ought to	
▨ discount	▨ sore throat	▨ show	**Expressions**
▨ fever	▨ swim	(someone)	▨ eat right
▨ headache	▨ upset stomach	around	▨ in good/bad
▨ health club	▨ yoga	▨ swim	shape
▨ lane			

Check (✓) the things you did in this chapter. How well can you do each one?

	Very well	Fairly well	Not very well
I can listen to and practice using stressed words.	☐	☐	☐
I can listen to and use tag questions.	☐	☐	☐
I can talk about health and stress.	☐	☐	☐
I can take notes on a conversation.	☐	☐	☐
I can summarize my notes.	☐	☐	☐
I can guess meanings from context.	☐	☐	☐
I can ask for and give advice.	☐	☐	☐
I can practice making a doctor's appointment.	☐	☐	☐

Write what you learned and what you liked in this chapter.

In this chapter,

I learned _____

_____

I liked _____

_____

8 Entertainment and the Media

Whoever controls the
media—the images—
controls the culture.

Allen Ginsberg
American poet

In this
CHAPTER

Conversation Watching TV

News Report An Airplane Crash

Getting Meaning from Context Advertisements

Real-World Tasks Talking About TV Shows

Connecting to the Topic

1. Look at the photo of a reality TV program. Who are the people in the photo? How do they feel?

2. What TV programs do you enjoy watching? Why?

3. What are some of your favorite advertisements? Why?

Watching TV

Before You Listen

1 **Prelistening Questions** Before you listen, talk about television with a partner.

1. How many hours of TV do you watch a week?

2. How many television sets do you have in your house? Where are they?

3. In your opinion, what's the best way to get the news: from television, a newspaper, or the Internet? Why?

4. Look at the photo. What is Jack doing? How do you know? What is Ming doing?

▲ How does Jack like to relax? What is Ming thinking?

2 Previewing Vocabulary Listen to the words and phrases from the conversation. Then complete the sentences with the words and phrases. Don't write anything on the lines on the left. You will use those lines in Activity 8.

Nouns	Verbs
average week	change channels
couch potato	channel surf
remote control	turn down the volume
the TV	turn on the TV
waste of time	turn the TV off

1. _____ As soon as I get home from work, I _____ _____ because I want to know what's on the news.

2. _____ When friends come to visit, we usually _____ _____ and just talk.

3. _____ When I don't like a TV show, I _____ _____ and find another program.

4. _____ The commercials are very loud, so I _____ _____ when they come on.

5. _____ I prefer to study in a quiet room, without _____ on.

6. _____ To find a good program on TV, I don't look in the newspaper. I usually just _____ until I find something interesting.

7. _____ I don't like to exercise or go out; I prefer to stay home and watch TV. I guess I am a _____.

8. _____ It's easy to change channels with a _____ _____.

9. _____ I think TV is very entertaining and educational, but other people think it's a _____.

10. _____ I watch 20 hours of TV during a(n) _____ _____.

Listen

3 Listening for Main Ideas Ming is visiting Jack. They are talking about television. Close your book and listen to the conversation. Listen for the answers to these questions.

1. What do Jack and Ming think about watching TV? Do they agree or disagree?

2. Why does Ming prefer to get the news from the Internet or the newspaper?

3. What is Jack's habit when watching TV?

Compare and discuss your answers with a partner.

4 **Listening for Details** Listen again if necessary. Write *T* if a statement is true and *F* if it is false.

1. _____ The average American watches five hours of TV a day.

2. _____ Ming is reading a newspaper.

3. _____ Ming is a couch potato.

4. _____ Jack doesn't like soap operas.

5. _____ Ming and Jack don't like TV commercials.

Stress

5 **Listening for Stressed Words** Listen to the conversation again. Some of the stressed words are missing. During each pause, repeat the phrase or sentence. Then fill in the blanks with the words you hear.

Ming: Hey, _____ to this. The _____ American watches _____ hours of TV a day.

Jack: A day? You're _____.

Ming: No, it says so right here in this _____. Hmm, I guess _____ an average American, Jack. You _____ have your _____ on.

Jack: Come on. Are you saying I'm a _____ potato?

Ming: Yeah. I really think watching TV is a _____ of time.

Jack: Oh, come _____. _____ programs are bad, like those _____ operas. But what about sports or the _____? You watch those sometimes, don't you?

Ming: Well, actually, for the _____, I prefer the _____. Or the _____.

Jack: Why?

Ming: First, because they give you a lot more _____. And I can _____ them any time I want. Plus, I _____ all the commercials.

Jack: I know what you _____. That's why, when the commercials come on, I just _____ down the volume or change _____.

Ming: Yeah, I noticed that. Channel surfing drives me _____.

Jack: Okay, next time you come _____, I'll let you have the

remote _____.

Ming: Oh, that's so sweet. But I have a _____ idea. Next time

I come over, let's just turn the TV _____.

Now read the conversation with a partner. Practice stressing words correctly.

Reductions

6 **Comparing Unreduced and Reduced Pronunciation** The following sentences come from the conversation. Listen for the difference between unreduced and reduced pronunciation. Repeat both forms after the speaker.

Unreduced Pronunciation	**Reduced Pronunciation***
1. Are you saying I'm a couch potato?	<u>Arya</u> saying I'm a couch potato?
2. You watch those sometimes, don't you?	You watch those sometimes, <u>dontcha</u>?
3. I know what you mean.	I know <u>whatcha</u> mean.
4. I'll let you have the remote control.	I'll <u>letcha</u> have the remote control.

* Note: The underlined forms are not acceptable spellings in written English.

7 **Listening for Reductions** Two friends are talking about seeing a movie at the campus theater. Listen to the following sentences. You'll hear the reduced pronunciation of some words. Repeat each sentence during the pause. Then write the unreduced forms of the missing words in the blanks.

A: _____ _____ calling the movie theater?

B: Uh-huh. _____ _____ _____

_____ go to the movies tonight?

A: To tell _____ the truth, I'm pretty tired. But we _____

go to an early show. _____ _____ know

_____ _____ _____

_____ see?

B: Not really. I'll _____ _____ choose. *Batman III* is

playing at eight and James Bond is at ten.

A: Let's see *Batman III.* I'm tired now and by ten o'clock I'm _____

_____ be dead.

With a partner, read the conversation. Practice the reduced pronunciation.

8 Using Vocabulary Look at the ten statements in Activity 2 on page 145. In the blanks on the left, check (✓) the sentences that are true for you. With a partner, discuss the sentences that are *not* true for you. Use the new vocabulary in your discussion.

Example

Number 6 is not true in my case. I don't like to <u>channel surf</u>. Before I <u>turn on the TV</u>, I always choose a program from the TV guide. But my brother <u>channel surfs</u> all the time.

"Would you please pick something and quit channel surfing."

Drawing by Frascino; © 1979. The New Yorker Magazine. Inc. The New Yorker Collection 1994
Leo Cullum from cartoonbank.com. All Rights Reserved.Reprinted by permission.

Using Language Functions

FOCUS

Expressing Opinions, Agreeing, and Disagreeing

When Ming and Jack had different opinions about television, they used the following language:

Ming: I really think watching TV is a waste of time.

Jack: Oh, come on!

Look at other expressions English speakers use to express opinions, to agree, and to disagree.

9 **Expressing Opinions** Work in groups of three. Look at the nine topics below. Take turns giving your opinion on each topic like this:

Student A: Give your opinion about the topic. Give reasons.
Student B: Agree or disagree. Give reasons.
Student C: Agree or disagree with A or B. Give reasons.

Example

Ming: I think watching TV is a waste of time. Most programs are stupid or boring.

Jack: I disagree with you. Many programs are useful—if you choose them carefully.

Peter: I agree with Ming. There are so many better things to do than sit and watch TV.

1. violence on television
2. getting movies and music for free on the Internet
3. magazine stories about private lives of famous people
4. high salaries of superstar athletes
5. high salaries of movie stars
6. low salaries of teachers
7. government control of television programs (censorship)
8. high price of rock concert tickets
9. (choose your own topic)

PART 2 News Report

An Airplane Crash

Before You Listen

Strategy

Graphic Organizer: Four (Five) Ws
To take notes on an event, use a four (or five) Ws graphic organizer. Write questions about the situation asking *what, where, when, who,* (and possibly *why*). The answers to these four (or five) questions will give you a complete picture of the event.

1 **Prelistening Questions** Before you listen, talk about accidents with a partner.

1. Have you ever seen an accident? Describe what happened.

2. Imagine a news report about an airplane crash. Write four questions about it in the Four Ws Graphic Organizer:

	Question
What	?
Where	?
When	?
Who	?

2 **Previewing Vocabulary** Listen to the underlined words from the conversation. You will hear the underlined words in a news report. Then, write the letter of the correct definition beside each sentence.
(Note: Two of the words have very similar meanings!)

Sentences

1. _____ What was the top story on the evening news last night?

2. _____ The airplane left Chicago at 3:00 and landed in San Francisco at 8:00.

3. _____ My sports car is so small, I can only take one passenger.

4. _____ He had two serious injuries: a broken arm and a broken knee.

5. _____ She had to go to the hospital because she was hurt in the accident.

6. _____ Dina's car broke down on the highway and blocked traffic for an hour.

7. _____ I ran out of money, so I asked my parents for $100.

Definitions

a. person in the car other than the driver

b. had no more

c. stopped something from moving

d. places where the body is damaged

e. the first story in a news program

f. experienced pain or damage to the body

g. arrived; touched the ground

3 Listening for Main Ideas Listen to a news report about an airplane crash.

▲ A news report about an airplane crash.

1. As you listen, write the key words in the space provided.

_____

_____

_____

_____

2. Which of the following is the main idea of the story?

   Ⓐ An airplane crashed onto the highway and everyone died.

   Ⓑ Two people saw the airplane crash and called the police.

   Ⓒ An airplane landed on the highway.

4 Listening for Specific Information Listen again. This time, take notes about the following details.

1. Location of the plane: _____

2. Number of passengers: _____

3. Number of passengers injured: _____

4. Type of injuries: _____

_____

5. Number of people injured on the ground: _____

6. Possible cause of crash: _____

_____

5 Summarizing Ideas Compare notes with a partner. Together, summarize the news report in your own words. As you speak, use your questions from Activity 1 and your notes from Activities 3 and 4 to help you remember the story.

6 Using Vocabulary Discuss the following questions with a partner. Use the underlined vocabulary in your answers.

1. Did you watch the news on TV last night? What was the top story?
2. If an airplane can't land because of bad weather, what can the pilot do?
3. On a long car trip, do you prefer to be the passenger or the driver? Why?
4. Tell about some injuries you had when you were a child. Were you hurt while playing or while doing sports? Were you seriously hurt?
5. If you run out of money while on vacation, what can you do?
6. How do you feel when someone blocks traffic unnecessarily?

Talk It Over

7 Summarizing News Reports Watch a news program online or on TV the day before your class. Choose one of the reports in the news. Give the class a short summary of the report. Use simple words and focus on the key ideas only. Use the Five Ws graphic organizer below. Write questions and answers in it and use it during your presentation.

	Question	Answer
What	?	
Where	?	
When	?	
Who	?	
Why	?	

Getting Meaning from Context

FOCUS ON TESTING

TOEFL® iBT

Using Context Clues

Many tests such as the TOEFL® iBT measure your academic listening and speaking abilities. This activity, and others in the book, will develop your social and academic communication abilities, and provide a foundation for success on a variety of standardized tests. You will hear five commercials. Decide which product or service they advertise.

1. Listen to the beginning of each commercial. Then listen to the question.

2. Stop the recording after each question and choose the product or service advertised.

3. In the **Clues** column, write the words that helped you choose your answer.

4. Listen to the last part of the commercial to hear the correct answer.

Answers	Clues
1. (A) soup (B) breakfast cereal (C) vitamins	
2. (A) long-distance calling plan (B) sleeping pill (C) cell phone company	
3. (A) baby products (B) a used car (C) a new car	
4. (A) breakfast food (B) TV magazine (C) sleeping pill	
5. (A) comedy show (B) daytime TV drama (C) TV news program	

1 **Discussing Advertisements** In small groups, discuss the qualities of a good advertisement. Make a list.

1. _It should be easy to notice._

2. _It should be funny, so we pay attention and remember it._

3. _____

4. _____

5. _____

Look at the following advertisement. Does it have all the qualities you just listed? Discuss what you like and don't like about this ad.

◀ What is this advertisement for? Would you buy this product? Why or why not?

Bring examples of an interesting and a boring ad from a magazine or newspaper to class. Explain to your classmates why you chose these ads.

Talking About TV Shows

1 **Types of TV Programs** Look at the types of television programs below. Give an example of each.

Types of Shows	Examples
a. reality show	*Survivor*
b. cartoon	
c. game show	
d. drama series	
e. sitcom (situation comedy)	
f. children's program	
g. news program	
h. soap opera	

Look at the list of popular TV shows from the United States and England. Match them with the types of shows above. Write the letters of the type of show on the lines. If you don't know some of the shows, find information about them online. What other popular shows do you know? Write their names in the chart above.

1. __g__ *CNN® International*
2. _____ *30 Rock*
3. _____ *Yo Gabba Gabba*
4. _____ *Mad Men*
5. _____ *Who Wants to Be a Millionaire?*
6. _____ *The Simpsons*
7. _____ *So You Think You Can Dance?*

2 **Discussing a Program Guide** Jennifer and her brother want to watch TV tonight. Before you listen, look at the page from the TV guide on page 157 and answer these questions:

1. What's on Channel 2 at 7:00?

2. What time is the news on? What channels is it on?

3. Who will be the guests on the *Oprah Winfrey* show?

Now listen to the conversation. During each pause, fill in the missing information and circle the type of program. Compare your answers with classmates.

PRIME-TIME WEDNESDAY						
Channel	7:00 PM	7:30 PM	8:00 PM	8:30 PM	9:00 PM	9:30 PM
2 KCBS	Survivor Reality show		America's Next Top Model Reality show		39th Annual Country Music Awards Award show	
4 NBC	Extra! Entertainment news magazine		The Apprentice Reality show		Law and Order Crime drama	
7 KABC	_____ (name of program) Game show/news/cartoon		The Oprah Winfrey Show Special guests: celebrity couples Talk show		News	
11 KTTV	30 Rock Comedy	30 Rock Comedy	_____ (name of program) Soap opera/talk show/movie			
13 KCOP	The Simpsons Comedy	King of the Hill Comedy	_____ (name of program) Movie/news/cartoon			
20 TLC	Alias Crime drama		_____ (name of program) Horror movie/drama series/soap opera			
CNN	Asia Today News show		Live from Washington News show	News	Anderson Cooper Live Talk show	
25 ESPN	NFL Live Sports		Sports Center Sportd news		_____ (name of program) Documentary/talk show/sports	
53 FX	Parks and Recreation Comedy		_____ (name of program) Cartoon/ children's show/sitcom	How I Met Your Mother Comedy	Mission Impossible Action adventure	The Bachelor Reality show

3 **Describing a Favorite Show or Movie** Tell a partner about your favorite TV show or movie. To help you organize your description, make notes about the points listed below.

1. Kind of show (drama, talk show, comedy, etc.):

_____

2. Type of people in it (young, single people; married couple; etc.):

_____

3. Situation (city police station, apartment building, etc.):

_____

4. Reasons you like it (funny characters, exciting story, educational, etc.):

_____

Example

I like to watch *Desperate Housewives*. It's a kind of soap opera about four housewives. They live in a very nice neighborhood and have different types of families and personalities. Each episode tells some secret about the housewives and their neighbors. I like the show because sometimes it's funny and other times it's very dramatic. I watch it every week to see what happens to the characters and how the housewives solve their problems.

▲ A scene from *Desperate Housewives,* an American TV show

Self-Assessment Log

Check (✓) the words you learned in this chapter.

Nouns
- average week
- couch potato
- injury
- passenger
- remote control
- top story
- the TV
- waste of time

Verbs
- block
- change channels
- channel surf
- hurt
- land
- run out of
- turn down the volume
- turn on the TV
- turn the TV off

Check (✓) the things you did in this chapter. How well can you do each one?

	Very well	Fairly well	Not very well
I can listen to and practice stress and reductions.	☐	☐	☐
I can express my opinions.	☐	☐	☐
I can take notes on a news report.	☐	☐	☐
I can summarize my notes.	☐	☐	☐
I can guess meanings from context.	☐	☐	☐
I can talk about TV shows and advertisements.	☐	☐	☐

Write what you learned and liked in this chapter.

In this chapter,

I learned _____

_____

I liked _____

_____

9 Social Life

> **"**A friend to all is a
> friend to none.**"**
>
> Greek proverb

In this
CHAPTER

Conversation Making a Date

Conversation Arranging a Match

Getting Meaning from Context At a Party

Real-World Tasks Making Social Plans

Connecting to the Topic

1. Look at the photo. Where are these people?
   What are they doing?

2. What types of activities do you like to do with your friends?

3. What are the qualities of a good friend?

Making a Date

1 **Prelistening Questions** Talk about your oldest friends with a partner.

1. Look at the photo. Have Ming and Yolanda seen Dan recently? Did they expect to see him?

2. How long have you known your closest friends? Since elementary school? Middle school? High school? College? After college?

3. Have you ever had a *reunion* with old friends? What did you talk about? Did you stay in touch after that?

4. Have you ever run into an old friend by accident? Where and when?

▲ Ming and Yolanda run into Dan on the street.

2 Previewing Vocabulary Listen to the words and expressions from the conversation. Complete the sentences below the chart and on page 164 with the words and expressions. Then write the examples and the meanings of the expressions in the chart.

Words and Expressions	Use of Words and Expressions in the Sentences	Meanings as Used Here
good at	"He has always been good at science."	He's able to understand science easily.
graduation		
keep in touch		
make sense		
on the road		
pre-med		
sales rep		
terrific		
(be) up to		

1. Dan plans to become a doctor because he has always been

   _____ science.

2. **Ming:** Hi, Dan. I haven't seen you in a while. What have you been

   _____ ?

   Dan: Not much. Just studying and going to school.

3. I love your new haircut. It really looks _____ .

4. I'm _____ most of the time because my company needs

   me to travel a lot.

5. Yolanda wants to go to medical school after college, so she's studying

   _____ courses in college now.

6. I send an email to my friends every week because I want to

   _____ with them.

7. To celebrate my _____ from high school, my parents bought me a new computer. It will be great to have a new computer when I go to college in the fall.

8. It doesn't _____ to buy a car if you live five minutes from your university.

9. **Ming:** I took this job because I am really good at selling things!

   Dan: Oh! So you're a _____ ?

3 **Listening for Main Ideas** Dan is visiting his hometown. He runs into two of his high school classmates walking down the street. Close your book and listen to the conversation. Prepare to answer these questions.

1. What is the main thing the three friends discuss?
2. Dan says he's been studying hard. What do the women think?
3. At the end of the conversation, what do the friends say they will do?

Compare and discuss your answers with a partner.

4 **Listening for Details** Listen to the conversation again if necessary. Answer these questions.

1. When was the last time Dan saw Yolanda and Ming?
2. What is Dan's major?
3. Ming is a sales rep. What is Yolanda studying in college?

Stress

5 **Listening for Stressed Words** Listen to the conversation again. Some of the stressed words are missing. During each pause, repeat the phrase or sentence. Then fill in the blanks with words you hear.

Yolanda: Ming, look! I can't _____ it! It's Dan. Hey Dan! How are you?

Dan: Yolanda? Ming? Wow! I haven't seen you guys since _____ night!

Ming: I know. You look _____ !

Dan: Thanks. So do _____ !

Ming: So what have you been _____ to?

Dan: Well, I go to Faber College.

Yolanda: _____ ? Do you _____ it?

Dan: Yeah, _____ _____. But I've been _____ really hard.

Ming: _____ you have…

Yolanda: So, what's your major?

Dan: It's _____ science.

Ming: Ah-h-h. _____ makes sense. You always _____ good at _____ and _____.

Dan: Thanks. Anyway, what have _____ guys been up to?

Ming: Well, I'm a _____ rep for a publishing company.

Dan: No _____! How do you like that?

Ming: Oh, I _____ it! I'm on the road a lot, but I get to meet some interesting people.

Dan: That's _____. And how about _____, Yolanda?

Yolanda: I'm studying _____ at State College.

Dan: Wow—you can be my doctor! You always were _____ at science too. Well, it was great seeing you both. Let's keep in _____ from now on. Email me sometime. Here's my address.

Now read the conversation with two classmates. Practice stressing words correctly.

After You Listen

6 **Using Vocabulary** Discuss the following questions with a partner. Use the underlined vocabulary in your answers.

1. What have you <u>been up to</u> (during the past year)—besides studying English?

2. Tell about a restaurant that is a <u>terrific</u> place to go on a date, in your opinion. Why is it so great?

3. Tell about something your friends or family might think you are <u>good at</u>.

4. Do you <u>keep in touch</u> with any of your friends or teachers from when you were younger? Who?

5. Would you like a job that required you to be <u>on the road</u> 50 percent of the time?

6. Give several reasons why it <u>makes sense</u> or doesn't <u>make sense</u> for students to wear uniforms in school.

Pronunciation

FOCUS

Intonation with Exclamations

To express strong feelings (surprise, anger, happiness), we use exclamations. These are expressions that we pronounce with especially strong emphasis and with falling intonation at the end.

Wow!

No kidding!

Examples

Wow!   That's great!   I can't believe it!   That's awful!

7 **Pronouncing Exclamations** Listen and repeat the following exclamations from the conversation. Follow the stress and intonation patterns carefully.

1. Ming, look!
2. I can't believe it!
3. Wow! I haven't seen you guys since graduation night!
4. You look great!
5. So do you!
6. No kidding!
7. That's terrific!

8 Matching Statements and Responses Listen to these eight statements or questions. Choose the appropriate responses from the box and write their letters in the blanks below. Use a different exclamation each time.

a. That's amazing! How's she doing?
b. Congratulations!
c. That's great! I knew you could do it.
d. That's disgusting!
e. No way!
f. You're kidding! What did you talk about?
g. Not again!
h. Oh no! That's awful!

1. _a_
2. ____
3. ____
4. ____
5. ____
6. ____
7. ____
8. ____

9 Practicing Exclamations Work in pairs. Student A should look at page 202. Student B should look at page 206.

Using Language Functions

FOCUS

Giving and Accepting Compliments

In many places, or cultures, people give compliments to make other people feel comfortable, to be friendly, or to start a conversation. Look at these examples of giving and accepting compliments.

Giving Compliments	Accepting Compliments
Maria, your English is really improving.	Thanks. You're very kind.
Excuse me. Who cut your hair? I really like it. I love the way you sing, Henry.	Thank you.
You have a beautiful home, Mrs. Johnson.	So do you./You do too.

10 **Giving and Accepting Compliments** Practice giving and accepting compliments with your classmates as follows: Student A gives a compliment to Student B. Student B accepts the compliment and gives a compliment to Student C. Continue until everyone has given and received a compliment. Here are some topics you can give people compliments on:

1. an item of clothing or jewelry
2. a hairstyle
3. something someone did
4. a change or improvement someone made recently
5. something a person does well

Arranging a Match

Before You Listen

 1 **Prelistening Questions** Before you listen, talk about social life and dating with a classmate.

1. Is dating common in your culture or circle of friends? If yes, how do you meet people to go on a date? If no, explain how you like to socialize with friends.
2. What do you think of "blind dates"? Do you know anyone who has gone on a blind date?
3. If you marry, how do you think you might meet your husband or wife?
4. Do you believe in love at first sight?
5. What are the most important qualities or characteristics to look for in a husband or wife?
6. Would you trust your family members (parents or brothers and sisters) to select a husband or wife for you? Why or why not?

Listen

 2 **Listening for Main Ideas** Listen to the conversation between Tanya and Meena. As you listen to their conversation, answer the following questions.

1. What does Tanya want to do for her friend Meena?
2. Why does Meena say no to Tanya's suggestion?
3. Does Tanya seem interested in learning about Meena's culture?

3 **Taking Notes on Specific Information** Listen to the conversation again. This time, take notes about Meena's culture and its views on dating and marriage.

Ways to meet a husband: _____

_____

For Meena, the right man must be: _____

_____

_____

Meena's view on love: _____

_____

Possible advantages of this kind of marriage: _____

_____

After You Listen

4 **Summarizing Ideas** Work with a partner. Take turns explaining Meena's beliefs about a good marriage match. Use your notes from Activity 3 to help you.

5 **Discussing Dating Customs** Work in small groups. Talk about dating customs. Think about your own or your friends' experiences. Explain your answers.

1. In cultures where dating is popular, what age do you think is right for boys or girls to start dating?

2. Is it OK to ask someone you have just met out on a date?

3. Where do couples (married or dating) in your culture go out together: to a movie? a restaurant? a nightclub? a concert?

4. When a couple goes out, who usually pays? Who should pay?

5. Do you think it is a good thing to date many different people before you get married? Why or why not?

6. What do you think are some of the most usual, or unusual, ways or places that people in different cultures meet their future husbands or wives?

Culture Note

Dating in North America
When two people who have romantic feelings for each other go out together, their meeting is called a date. In the U.S. and Canada, boys and girls start dating around age 15. Often, people who are dating first meet at school, at work, at a sports or music event, at a party, at a club, or online. Once in a while, a friend or relative arranges a date, and people meet for the first time at the time of the date. This is called a blind date.

6 **Meeting Friends and Dates Online** Imagine that you just met the following six attractive single people at a party. Each wants to find someone to date. You are the "matchmaker." Read the notes on page 171 about each person carefully. In small groups, talk about which pairs might make a good or bad match, and why.

Women	Men
Lisa—22	**Ritchie—25**
Majored in biology; studied one year in Australia.	Law major; very busy in new job at big law firm.
Part-time job in pharmacy now, might continue for a masters degree.	Under a lot of stress
Independent, confident, funny.	Likes tennis, and just started playing golf.
Loves shopping for expensive shoes.	Enjoys spicy foods.
Marta—23	**Mo—24**
Studied art history; is a photographer who works for a magazine.	Business major; might start MBA soon.
Loves the mountains and hiking.	Family has small export business.
Vegetarian who likes cooking healthy meals.	Serious—a bit old fashioned.
Loves films, dancing, and travel.	Likes privacy and quiet places.
Very easygoing.	His mother often cooks for him.
Anna—21	**Frank—23**
Accounting major with job offers at two strong companies.	Communications major, but is now learning animation.
Shy, but friendly and kind.	Part-time DJ, loves international dance open space music—doesn't earn much money.
Likes reading and jogging.	Likes trying new foods, but eats a lot of junk food when busy.
Gets take-out dinners often.	Loves biking and the outdoors.

7 Filling Out a Questionnaire

Online dating services try to help people find interesting people to date. New members usually create a profile to explain who they are and what kind of person they'd like to meet. Then the service prepares a list of matches for them to look over and contact (or not).

Pretend that you are going to sign up with an online dating service, and follow these instructions.

1. Fill out the profile, but don't write your real name at the top. Use an imaginary name. **You can answer truthfully, or have fun and make up pretend answers.** Your teacher will collect all the profiles and put them on the board or wall.

2. The women in the class will read the profiles from the men, and the men will read the profiles from the women.

3. Choose the profile of the person who seems the most interesting to you.

4. The teacher will point to each profile and ask, for example, "This application is from Mr. Cool. Can you all guess who this is?" (Students try to guess.) "Would you like to meet him? Well let's meet him now."

5. Finally, "Mr. Cool" will stand up and reveal his identity.

6. Repeat steps 4 and 5 for all the profiles.

FindYourMatch.com

'User Name' (<u>not</u> real name) _____ Age: _____ ❏ Male ❏ Female

DETAILS ABOUT ME:

School major or favorite class _____

Future plans or dreams (be accountant at big company, open a restaurant, get married and have

children, etc.): _____

_____

_____

Good habits (very loyal, exercise daily, etc.): _____

_____

Bad habits (eat junk food, step on toes when dancing, etc.): _____

_____

Finish these sentences:

My friends say I am very… a. _____ b. _____

Two things that make me happy are… a. _____ b. _____

Two things that make me angry are… a. _____ b. _____

My hobbies and interests include… (video games, tennis, rap music, etc.)

_____

Three things I can't live without are: (nice shoes, my cat, travel, religion, etc.)

1. _____ 2. _____ 3. _____

MY FUTURE DATE:

Should be _____ to _____ years old, and have these…:

Future plans or dreams (finish college, be president of a big company, open

a restaurant, get married and have children, make a lot of money, make a movie, etc.):

_____

_____

_____

_____

_____

_____

_____

Good habits: (very loyal, exercise daily, etc.): _____

_____

_____

_____

(Not have these) Bad habits: (eat junk food, watch too much TV, etc.):

_____

_____

_____

_____

Hobbies and interests such as (jazz music, cooking, snowboarding, etc.):

_____

_____

_____

_____

_____

Getting Meaning from Context

FOCUS ON TESTING

TOEFL® iBT

Using Context Clues

Many tests such as the TOEFL® iBT measure your academic listening and speaking abilities. This activity, and others in the book, will develop your social and academic communication abilities, and provide a foundation for success on a variety of standardized tests. Listen to five conversations that take place at a party.

1. Listen to the first part of each conversation. Then listen to the question.
2. Stop the recording and choose the best answer to each question.
3. In the **Clues** column, write the words that helped you choose your answer.
4. Start the recording again. Listen to the last part of the conversation to hear the correct answer.

Answers	Clues
1. Ⓐ The man doesn't like the town. Ⓑ The man is new in town. Ⓒ The woman used to live in the town.	
2. Ⓐ The office manager hurt his neck. Ⓑ The man works with the woman. Ⓒ The man and woman used to work together.	
3. Ⓐ The woman doesn't want to go out with the man. Ⓑ The woman never eats lunch. Ⓒ The man is going to call the woman this weekend.	
4. Ⓐ The man is worried about Tony. Ⓑ The woman is worried about Tony. Ⓒ Tony went home.	
5. Ⓐ The man and the woman will leave the party in forty-five minutes. Ⓑ The man and woman had a misunderstanding. Ⓒ The man and woman came to the party together.	

1 **Discussing Parties** Answer the following questions with a small group.

1. Describe a typical, enjoyable party for people in your age group. Think of the kind of parties you might go to. Include the following information:

   a. Where is the party held?

   b. What time does the party start?

   c. What food is served?

   d. What do people drink?

   e. What kind of entertainment is there?

   f. Do you bring a gift for the host?

   g. When does the party end?

2. Why do you think some young people drink, or like to get drunk? What is your opinion of this activity?

3. If someone drinks alcohol at a party, how does that person get home?

4. The poster below is from an advertising campaign from the state of Connecticut (CT). Have you seen posters of advertisements like this before? Do posters like this stop people from drinking and driving? Why or why not?

Making Social Plans

1 Prelistening Discussion Look at the advertisements for entertainment below and on page 177. Answer the questions in a small group.

1. What type of entertainment is each poster advertising?

> a movie   a pop music concert
> a classical music concert   a nightclub (or dance club)
> an opera

2. Discuss which of these things you might like to do tonight. Decide on one activity with your group.

3. Discuss which activity you chose with the class.

2 Previewing Vocabulary You will hear the underlined words in some phone conversations and messages. Listen to the underlined words. Then use the context presented here to guess what the words mean. Write a definition or description in the spaces.

Sentences	Definitions
1. **A:** What's showing at the Coronet theater tonight? **B:** A <u>sci-fi</u> movie with Tom Cruise. **A:** Tom Cruise in a sci-fi movie—sounds exciting! What are the <u>show times</u>? **B:** 4, 7, and 10.	sci-fi movie: show times:
2. **A:** Want to go see some <u>live music</u> at the Sunset Grill tonight? **B:** Who's singing? **A:** A woman named Sarah Waggoner. She's supposed to be great. **B:** OK. What does it cost? **A:** There's a <u>cover charge</u> of 15 dollars and you have to buy at least two drinks. **B:** Sorry, that's too expensive for me.	live music: cover charge:
3. When you buy tickets to entertainment events online, you often have to pay a <u>service charge</u> of two dollars or more. If you order tickets by phone, you can get them in the mail or you can pick them up at the <u>box office</u> before the event begins.	service charge: box office:
4. If you want to have dinner at a well-known restaurant, it's best to <u>make a reservation</u> before you go. If you don't have a reservation, you may have to wait for a long time when you get there.	make a reservation:

With a partner, role-play Conversations 1 and 2.

3 Taking Notes Jack and Ming plan to go out this weekend. Ming is making phone calls to get more information about three events. Listen to the calls and take notes on the important information.

Call 1

Event: _____

Location: _____

Show time(s): _____

Price of tickets: _____

Call 2

Place: _____

Entertainment tonight: _____

Cost: _____

Menu: _____

Reservations: _____   _____
                          Number of people   Time

Call 3

Place: _____

Band: _____

Date: _____

Price (total): _____

Remember to bring: _____

4 Using Vocabulary Discuss the following questions with a partner. Use the underlined vocabulary in your answers.

1. Do you like sci-fi (science fiction) movies? Give an example of a sci-fi movie you enjoyed.

2. Do you ever go to nightclubs to hear live music? Talk about the last time you went. What was the cover charge to get into the club? Did you have to make a reservation?

3. Have you ever ordered tickets to an event by phone? What was the service charge? Did your tickets come by mail, or did you pick them up at the box office?

4. How can you find out the show times for an event you want to attend?

5 Role-Play Work in pairs. Student A should look at page 202. Student B should look at page 206. Follow the directions that go with the activity on those pages.

Self-Assessment Log

Check (✓) the words you learned in this chapter.

Nouns
- box office
- cover charge
- graduation
- live music
- pre-med
- sales rep
- sci-fi movie

- service charge
- show times

Verbs
- be up to
- keep in touch
- make a reservation
- make sense

Adjectives
- good at
- terrific

Expression
- on the road

Check (✓) the things you did in this chapter. How well can you do each one?

	Very well	Fairly well	Not very well
I can listen to and practice stress.	☐	☐	☐
I can talk about friends.	☐	☐	☐
I can express strong feelings with exclamations.	☐	☐	☐
I can give and accept compliments.	☐	☐	☐
I can take notes on a conversation.	☐	☐	☐
I can summarize my notes.	☐	☐	☐
I can talk about dating customs and parties.	☐	☐	☐
I can guess meanings from context.	☐	☐	☐
I can talk about going out to movies and clubs.	☐	☐	☐

Write what you learned and liked in this chapter.

In this chapter,

I learned _____

_____

I liked _____

_____

10 Sports

I've failed over and over and over again in my life and that is why I succeed.

Michael Jordan
American basketball player

In this **CHAPTER**

Conversation Explaining a Sport

Speech A Female Wrestler

Getting Meaning from Context Which Sport Is It?

Real-World Tasks Following Sports News

Connecting to the Topic

1 Look at the photo. What's happening?

2 What are your favorite sports to watch? Why?

3 What qualities do you think someone needs in order to become a successful athlete? Explain.

Explaining a Sport

Before You Listen

1 Prelistening Questions
Look at the photo. Answer the questions with a partner.

▲ A woman practicing Karate

1. What do you know about martial arts?
2. Why do people want to learn such sports?
3. What experience, if any, do you have with them?

2 Previewing Vocabulary Listen to the words and phrases from the conversation. Complete the sentences with the words and phrases.

Nouns	Verbs	
balance	focus	stretch
confidence	get in shape	warm up
flexibility	get into	

1. My uncle hasn't exercised for many years and he has gained a lot of weight.

   But now he wants to _____.

2. Some basketball players can jump and _____ their arms up to touch the basket.

3. Bicyclists need good _____ if they don't want to fall off their bikes.

4. Many young women who are shy often develop more _____ after they learn to play a sport well.

5. To do yoga or gymnastics, you need great _____ to move your body in difficult positions.

6. If you have a lot of fun doing a new sport, it's easy to _____ it.

7. To become a winner, you must concentrate your vision and effort in one

   direction. You really need to _____ on your goal.

8. Professional tennis players usually _____ for several minutes to get their bodies ready to start to play a match.

3 **Listening for Main Ideas** Ming, Peter, and Kenji are together to practice some martial arts. Close your book and listen to the conversation. Prepare to answer these questions:

1. What sport will Ming, Peter, and Kenji practice?
2. What part of the world does this sport come from?
3. What are some differences between the two sports they discuss?
4. How has this sport helped Ming?

Compare and discuss your answers with a partner.

◀ Kick

Block ▶

◀ Punch

4 Listening for Details Listen again if necessary. Write *T* if a statement is true and *F* if it is false.

1. _____ Ming is trying to teach her friends Karate.

2. _____ Tae Kwon Do uses more kicks than Karate does.

3. _____ Kenji doesn't have any experience with Karate.

4. _____ Peter isn't very interested in learning such sports.

Stress

5 Listening for Stressed Words Listen to the conversation again. Some of the stressed words are missing. During each pause, repeat the phrase or sentence. Then fill in the blanks with the words you hear.

Ming: OK guys. Let's _____ _____ and

_____. We've got to work on _____ and

_____.

Peter: So, Ming, when did you _____ _____ this

Karate stuff?

Kenji: Karate's _____. Ming's showing us Tae Kwon Do, and

it's Korean.

Peter: _____. So, what's the _____?

Ming: Tae Kwon Do uses _____ of different _____

moves. But Karate... well, Kenji, it sounds like _____ know

something about Karate.

Kenji: Yeah—Karate uses more _____ and _____,

too. Maybe you've seen guys break wooden _____ with

punches. You know, like... I learned _____ when I was

in _____.

Peter: That's _____. I wish _____ could do that.

So, Ming, why did you get into Tae Kwon Do?

Ming: I had a Korean friend in _____ school, and he said it could

help me get in _____ and _____ my

confidence. So I _____ it, and I really liked it.

Peter: It looks like you _____.

Now read the conversation with two other classmates. Practice stressing words correctly.

Reductions

Dropping the "H" Sound

The "h" sound is not pronounced when a word is:

unstressed AND in the middle of a phrase

or

unstressed AND at the end of a sentence

The "h" sound is often dropped in *pronouns*, and *have/has/had*.

Unreduced "h"	Dropped "h"
Has he won yet?	Has'e won yet?
I don't know how to find her.	I don't know how to find'er.

In the following examples, the "h" is not dropped because it is in a stressed word:
Can I **help** you? I **hope** so.

---

6 **Listening for the Dropped "H"** Listen to the following sentences. Repeat them after the speaker.

Unreduced Pronunciation

1. I don't know what to get her.
2. Give it to him.
3. Is he winning?
4. What's his team's name?
5. Where have you been?
6. Susan has finished her workout.
7. He helped her get tickets.

Dropped "h" Pronunciation*

1. I don't know what to get 'er.
2. Give it to 'im.
3. Is 'e winning?
4. What's 'is team's name?
5. Where 'uv you been?
6. Susan 'as finished 'er workout.
7. He helped 'er get tickets.

7 **Comparing Unreduced and Reduced Pronunciation** The following sentences come from the conversation. Listen for the difference between the unreduced and reduced pronunciation. Repeat both forms after the speaker.

Unreduced Pronunciation

1. We've got to work on balance.
2. Why did you get into Tae Kwon Do?
3. And he said it could help me…
4. It looks like you succeeded.
5. I'm still working on it.

Reduced Pronunciation*

We've gotta work on balance.

Why didja get into Tae Kwon Do?

An 'e said it could help me…

It looks likeya succeeded.

I'm still workin' on it.

* Note: The underlined forms are not acceptable spellings in written English.

8 Listening for Reductions Listen to the following conversation between roommates. You'll hear the reduced forms of some words. Repeat each sentence during the pause. Then write the unreduced forms of the missing words in the blanks.

Jane: Hi, Helen. Are _____ going out?

Helen: Yeah, I'm going to the football game. My brother's playing and
I thought I'd watch _____. Do you _____
_____ come?

Jane: I really can't… I _____ _____ study. But can
_____ do me a favor?

Helen: OK.

Jane: _____ _____ get me tickets for the girls' soccer
game next Saturday? My cousin Sue just made the team.

Helen: Sure—that's so cool. What's _____ position?

Jane: I'm not sure—I'm _____ _____ call
_____, and I can ask _____, if you want.

Helen: _____ don't have to—just wish _____ luck.

With a partner, read the conversation. Practice the reduced pronunciation.

After You Listen

9 Reviewing Vocabulary Discuss the following questions with a partner.
Use the new vocabulary in your discussion.

1. What's your favorite sport, or game, and how did you get into it?
2. Why is it important to warm up before beginning to play a game or match?
3. Which activity do you think helps you get in shape the best: going dancing, playing Ping-Pong, or racing cars?
4. What are a few sports for which you really need flexibility and you have to stretch a lot?
5. Can you think of a sport that especially requires very good focus and balance?
6. How can playing a sport build a person's confidence?

▲ Ping-pong paddles and ball

▲ Racing cars

▲ Going dancing

Pronunciation

The North American "T"

In some words, speakers of North American English pronounce the "t" between two vowels as a quick /d/ sound:

Karate's (<u>kerahdeez</u>) Japanese.

This pronunciation change does not happen in British English. Contrast:

Words	North American English Pronunciation	British English Pronunciation
pretty	pri<u>dd</u>y*	pri<u>tt</u>y*
got it	go<u>dd</u>it*	go<u>tt</u>it*

*Note that the words marked with * are not correct written forms.

10 Listening for the North American "T" Listen and repeat the following examples.

1. We've go<u>tt</u>a work on balance and flexibili<u>t</u>y. ("go<u>dd</u>a") ("flexibili<u>d</u>y")

2. I<u>t</u> also helps you focus. ("i<u>d</u>")

3. Let's ge<u>t</u> star<u>t</u>ed. ("star<u>d</u>ed")

11 Pronouncing the North American "T" Work in pairs. Student A should look at page 203. Student B should look at page 207. Follow the directions on those pages.

A Female Wrestler

Before You Listen

1 **Prelistening Questions** Before you listen, talk about sports with a partner.

1. Which sports are more popular among men than women? Why?

2. How much do you know about the sport of wrestling? For example, what are the rules, what are the different kinds of wrestling styles, etc?

2 **Previewing Vocabulary** Listen to the underlined words from the speech. Then write the letter of the correct definition beside each sentence.

Sentences

1. _____ Our soccer team competed against another team and won.

2. _____ My roommate and I played a tennis match and then watched a soccer match on TV.

3. _____ John was so happy because he beat his father at a card game.

4. _____ We lost the basketball game because our opponents played much better.

5. _____ Nobody scored during the game, so the result was 0:0.

6. _____ Since the game was tied 2:2, they had to play overtime until one team finally won.

7. _____ Swimming is a great sport because you can participate as an individual or as a team member.

Definitions

a. to win against another player

b. the other player or team in a competition

c. to make points in a sport or game

d. to play a sport and try to win

e. one person, not a member of a group

f. a game or contest

g. extra time added at the end of a sports game

3 **Taking Notes on Main Ideas** Listen to the speech. Take notes in the space below. Focus on the main ideas about the speaker and her sport.

▲ France's wrestler Anna Gomis (in blue) wrestles Ida Karlson from Switzerland.

Hints for Taking Notes

It is easier to remember information if you organize your notes into an *outline*. An outline separates main ideas and details in a clear way with numbers and letters. An outline has key words and phrases—not complete sentences.

4 **Reviewing Notes** Look at your notes in Activity 3. Separate the main ideas from the details and write them in the outline below.

I. Introduction

   A. Info about Terri: _____

   B. Info about wrestling: _____

II. Why she chose wrestling: _____

_____

III. Rules: _____

_____

_____

_____

IV. Why she likes it: _____

_____

5 **Listening for Specific Information** Listen again while you look at the outline. Make corrections or fill in missing information.

After You Listen

6 **Summarizing Ideas** Compare notes with a partner. Summarize the information in your outline. Based on your summary, work with a partner and role-play an imaginary interview with Terri.

Example

Reporter: When did you start wrestling?

Terri: When I was 12.

Reporter: Why did you choose this sport?

Terri: Because my brothers used to wrestle and I…

7 **Reviewing Vocabulary** Ask and answer the following questions with a partner. Use the underlined vocabulary in your answers.

1. Why do you think women wrestlers couldn't <u>compete</u> in the Olympics before 2004?

2. Do you prefer to compete in sports as an <u>individual</u> or as part of a team? Why?

3. In your opinion, should women compete only against each other or against both female and male <u>opponents</u> in the following sports? Why?

- swimming
- wrestling
- running
- soccer
- golf
- skiing

Using Language Functions

FOCUS

Talking About Sports

With some sports, you can add *-ing* or *-er* to describe the activity or the athlete.

Action (verb)	Sport (noun)	Person (noun)
wrestle	wrestling	wrestler
ice-skate	ice-skating	ice-skater
surf	surfing	surfer
box	boxing	boxer

Example *Surfing* is my favorite sport. I *surf* every summer. All my friends are *surfers*.

Some sports only have noun forms. These sports follow the verbs *play* or *do*.

Example play tennis   do gymnastics

          play volleyball   do karate

8 **Talking About Sports** Look at these photos. Describe each photo using the correct noun or verb.

Example These hockey players are playing hockey.

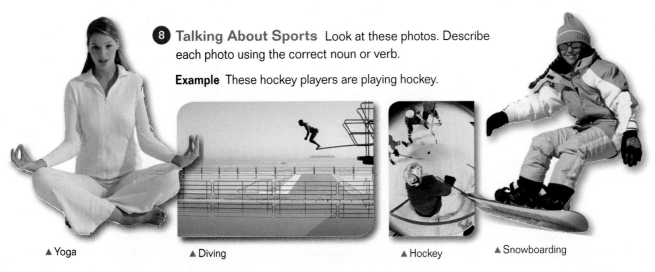

▲ Yoga   ▲ Diving   ▲ Hockey   ▲ Snowboarding

Sports   **191**

Getting Meaning from Context

1 **Prelistening Questions** Look at the pictures below. Name each sport and answer these questions with a partner.

1. Compare the sports in each group: How are they similar or different?
2. Which of these can you do without any equipment?
3. Which of these sports do you think is the oldest?

FOCUS ON TESTING

Using Context Clues

Many tests such as the TOEFL® iBT measure your academic listening and speaking abilities. This activity, and others in the book, will develop your social and academic communication abilities and provide a foundation for success on a variety of standardized tests. Listen to people describe various sports.

1. Listen to each description.
2. Stop the recording after each description.
3. Choose the best answer for each item.
4. In the **Clues** column, write the words that helped you.

Answers		Clues
1. (A)	swimming	
(B)	kayaking	
(C)	water skiing	

Answers	Clues
2. (A) judo	
(B) boxing	
(C) baseball	
3. (A) skiing	
(B) surfing	
(C) snowboarding	
4. (A) gymnastics	
(B) running	
(C) fencing	
5. (A) basketball	
(B) volleyball	
(C) baseball	

2 **Twenty Questions** Play the guessing game "Twenty Questions" by following these steps:

1. Divide into two teams.

2. Choose a player to represent your team. This person must think of a sport or a famous athlete.

3. Members of the other team ask Yes/No questions about the sport or athlete and try to guess the answer. Each member can ask one question and make one guess at his/her turn.

4. The player answers the questions with a simple Yes or No.

5. If the other team guesses the answer in 20 clues or less, it wins and gets one point.

6. The winning team selects a player for the next turn.

7. If a team can't guess in 20 questions (or guesses the wrong answer), the opposite team gets a point and can select another player to think of a sport or athlete.

Example

A: Is it a sport?

B: Yes.

A: Is it a winter sport?

B: No.

A: Do you need any special equipment?

B: Yes…

Following Sports News

1 Prelistening Questions Discuss these questions with a partner.

1. Which sports or games have you watched "live" at a stadium or other location? Which sports have you watched on television? Which way is better? Why?

2. Have you ever listened to a game on the radio? Is this enjoyable? Why or why not?

3. Do you follow any sports, teams, or players through television news, newspapers, magazines, or on the Internet? Explain.

2 Previewing Vocabulary Listen to the words below. Then test your understanding of the words. Working with a partner, describe or explain each picture by using the correct forms of the words under each picture. Check answers with classmates.

Nouns	Verbs	Adjective	Expressions
loser	lose/lost	close	It was a tie!
rival	win/won		It was a close game.
score			What was the score?
set			
tie			
winner			

▲ Win/won/winner
lose/lost/loser
rival

▲ a close game

3 **Sports News on the Radio** Look at the chart about sports. Listen to the Faber College radio sports reporters. As you listen, fill in the missing information you hear about each game or sport.

Sport	Players or Teams	Results / Scores
Men's basketball	Faber vs. State College	Faber lost: 76 – 72
	Faber vs. Hamilton College	
		Won all 3 games: 1: 2: 21 – 18 3:
Tennis	Mary Johnson vs. _____	
Tournament		
Tennis	_____ vs. Lisa Kim	
Women's soccer		

FOCUS

Giving and Understanding Instructions

When giving instructions, use signal words to make sure your explanation is clear.

Ask questions to make sure your listener understood you.

First,...
Start with...
Then,...
After that,...
The last step is...

Is this clear?
Did you get that?
Are you following me?

When following instructions, ask for clarification.

I'm lost.
I didn't get that.
Wait. Can you
say that again?
Would you
repeat that?

4 **Sports Instructions** Use the expressions from page 197 as you play these games.

Game 1

1. Form groups (3 to 5 students). Each group writes a set of simple instructions, or rules, for playing a sport or game.

   Example

   (surfing) First carry the board into the ocean... Then lie down on the surfboard... Next swim (or paddle) out to some waves... Turn around to the beach... Now wait for a big wave... Swim fast toward the beach. Finally, stand up on your surfboard.

2. Then cut up the instructions into separate sentences.

3. Give the mixed-up sentences to another group to put in the correct order.

4. When you're done, check the answers.

Game 2

1. Form groups (3 to 5 students). With your group, write a set of instructions for playing a sport. Memorize the instructions. Each group slowly tells the instructions to the other groups, *without saying the name of the sport.*

2. The group that guesses the name of the sport first wins 1 point. After each group has explained their sport, the group with the most points wins.

   Example

   First, throw the ball up. Then hit it with your paddle. Try to hit the ball onto the table, then over the net. Next, the other player tries to hit the ball back to you. Continue to hit the ball over the net. If you can't hit it over the net, and onto the table, then you might lose a point (Answer: Ping-Pong).

5 **Teaching or Coaching Your Classmates: Homework Project**

At Home:

Write down several simple steps for any sport you know. Practice explaining and showing these steps.

In Class:

If possible, bring in some sports equipment, like a ball or tennis racket, to help you describe your sport. Give instructions to try to teach your classmates the sport. Remember to check for understanding.

Learners: Remember to ask for help if instructions aren't clear.

Self-Assessment Log

Check (✓) the words you learned in this chapter.

Nouns
- balance
- confidence
- flexibility
- individual
- loser
- match
- opponent
- rival
- score
- set

- tennis match
- tie
- winner

Verbs
- beat
- compete
- focus
- get in shape
- get into

- lose
- score
- stretch
- warm up
- win

Adjective
- close

Adverb
- overtime

Expressions
- What was the score?
- It was a tie!
- It was a close game.

Check (✓) the things you did in this chapter. How well can you do each one?

	Very well	Fairly well	Not very well
I can listen to and practice stress and reductions.	☐	☐	☐
I can listen to and pronounce the North American "t."	☐	☐	☐
I can talk about sports.	☐	☐	☐
I can take notes on a speech.	☐	☐	☐
I can summarize my notes.	☐	☐	☐
I can guess meanings from context.	☐	☐	☐
I can give and understand instructions.	☐	☐	☐

Write what you learned and what you liked in this chapter.

In this chapter,

I learned _____

_____

I liked _____

_____

Chapter 1 Part 1

8 **Reviewing Vocabulary** page 8

Questions: Ask the following questions. Your partner will choose the best response from his or her box.

1. Do you think it is OK to <u>stop by</u> a friend's house without calling first?

2. If you have a problem with your roommate, is it a good idea to e-mail him, or is it better to speak to him <u>in person</u>?

3. Who do you usually <u>hang out</u> with on weekends?

Answers: Now change roles. Listen to your partner ask you three questions. Choose the correct response for each question.

a. I think a <u>suite</u> is better because it's larger and more comfortable!

b. <u>Juniors</u> take more difficult classes.

c. I'm too busy to sit down for lunch. I usually just <u>grab something</u>.

Chapter 2 Part 3

2 **Talking About Seasons** page 35

Student A				
	Winter	Spring	Summer	Fall
Months	December– February		June– August	
Weather		warm		cool
			humid	cloudy
			sunny	
	snowy			
	wet			
	gray			

8 Using Vocabulary page 88

Read the clues (definitions) to your partner. Ask him/her to guess the
vocabulary. Try different explanations until your partner gives the right answer.

1. Something that is at a specific place or address. Not in a separate location.
   (on-site)

2. A room that has washing machines and dryers. People bring their clothes to
   wash there. (laundry)

3. A place or a person that is open, free, not busy. (available)

4. Another name for an apartment. (unit)

5. The owner of a house or apartment who rents out his place. You pay rent to
   this person. (landlord)

3 Comparing Pictures page 99

▲ Picture A

9 Practicing Exclamations page 167

Read your partner one statement or question from the list below. Your partner will respond with an appropriate exclamation. Then your partner will read one of his or her statements, and you will respond with an appropriate exclamation. Take turns.

1. I got 100% on the last grammar test.

2. Do you like my new haircut?

3. Yesterday my dog was hit by a car.

4. I got free tickets to the _____ concert.

   (Fill in the name of a rock group.)

5. (Make your own statement or question.)

Chapter 9   Part 4

5 Role-Play page 178

1. Questions: You want to go to the movie *Gladiator Reborn*. Phone the theater and get some information about it. Your partner will choose the best response from his or her list.

   Useful expressions

   What time is _____ showing?   How long is the movie?

   When does _____ start?   What's the address of the theater?

   How much are the tickets?   Where can I park?

2. Answers: Now change roles. You work for Ticket Express, an agency that sells tickets for a variety of cultural events. Your partner will phone you to order tickets to the show *The Lion King* at the Greek Theater. Here is the information you will need:

   Show time: 8:30 P.M.

   Ticket prices: $20, $30, $50. The $20 tickets are sold out. There is a service charge of $2.50 for each ticket ordered by phone.

   Ticket pickup: At the box office one hour before show time.

   Useful expressions

   The show begins at...   There is a service charge...

   The (show) is sold out.   You can pick up your tickets at...

11 **Pronouncing the North American "T"** page 187

1. Questions: Ask the following questions. Your partner will answer with a word containing the North American "t":

   1. When are you going to see the basketball game?

   2. Where was the Mexican soccer match?

   3. Do you think that swimmer is beautiful?

   4. Should I buy this sweater?

   5. I called my tennis partner, but she isn't home. What should I do?

2. Answers: Now change roles. Listen to and answer your partner's questions with one of these words or phrases:

   a British sport   better   hit it   mail it in   I try to play golf.

Chapter 1　Part 1

8 Reviewing Vocabulary page 8

Answers: Listen to your partner ask you three questions. Choose the correct response for each question.

a. I hang out with my friends and classmates on weekends.

b. To be polite, it's better to call your friend before you stop by.

c. It's always better to discuss problems in person.

Questions: Now change roles. Ask the following questions. Your partner will choose the best response from his or her box.

1. Do you usually sit down for a hot lunch or do you just grab something?
2. Do you prefer a single dormitory room or a suite to share with other students?
3. Which students have more difficult classes: freshmen or juniors?

Chapter 2　Part 3

2 Talking About Seasons page 35

Student B				
	Winter	**Spring**	**Summer**	**Fall**
Months		March–May		September–November
Weather	cold		hot	
	rainy	cool		
	cloudy	rainy		windy
				rainy

8 Using Vocabulary page 88

Read the clues (definitions) to your partner. Ask him/her to guess the vocabulary. Try different explanations until your partner gives the right answer.

1. A public transportation company. You can use this service to travel inside a city, without a car. (bus line)

2. Another word for "need" or "must have." Someone says it's necessary to do something. (require)

3. Without beds, tables, chairs. Empty. (unfurnished)

4. You can get your money back after you pay for something. (refundable)

5. Money that you pay and don't get back if you damage a house. (security deposit)

Chapter 5 | **Part 4**

3 Comparing Pictures page 99

▲ Picture B

9 Practicing Exclamations page 167

Read your partner one statement or question from the list below. Your partner will respond with an appropriate exclamation. Then your partner will read one of his or her statements, and you will respond with an appropriate exclamation. Take turns.

1. Somebody stole my brand-new bicycle.

2. I got accepted for next year at _____.

    (Fill in the name of a university.)

3. What do you think of the food at _____?

    (Fill in the name of a terrible restaurant or place to eat.)

4. Today is my birthday.

5. (Make your own statement or question.)

5 Role-Play page 178

1. Answers: You work at the Sunset Theater. Your partner will call you for some ticket information. Use this information to answer your partner's questions. (If you don't know an answer, make something up.)

   Movie: *Gladiator Reborn*

   Location: Sunset Theater, at the corner of Sunset St. and King's Road

   Show times: 4, 7, and 10 P.M.

   Ticket prices: $6.00 before 5 P.M.; $10.00 after 5 P.M.

Useful expressions

There's a show at…	We're located at…
Show times are…	Tickets cost…

2. Questions: Now change roles. You are going to call Ticket Express, an agency that sells tickets to sports and cultural events. You want to buy two tickets to the show *The Lion King* at the Greek Theater on the night of August 10.

Useful expressions

I'd like to order…	Where can I pick up the tickets?
How much are the tickets?	What time does the show begin?
Do you have student tickets?	

11 Pronouncing the North American "T" page 187

1. **Answers:** Listen to and answer your partner's questions with a word or phrase containing the North American "t":

   pretty   call her later   try it on   Mexico City   Saturday

2. **Questions:** Now change roles. Ask your partner these questions:

   1. What do you try to do every weekend?

   2. What should I do with my completed application?

   3. What is the opposite of worse?

   4. What kind of game is cricket?

   5. What do players do with a golf ball?

Audioscript

CHAPTER 1

Academic Life Around the World

PART 1 Conversation: Meeting Classmates

3 **Listening for Main Ideas** page 5

4 **Listening for Details** page 6

5 **Listening for Stressed Words** page 6

Jack: Excuse me—Aren't you Ming? Ming Lee?

Ming: Uh… Yes—oh hi—you're Jack! Great to meet you in person.

Jack: You looked a little different online…

Ming: You too; you're taller.

Jack: Well, I was sitting down when we video chatted. So, um, have you met anybody else? I mean from the freshman Facebook group?

Ming: A few guys—not many. When did you get into town?

Jack: I got here today—still got boxes everywhere… Oh, and Ming, this is Peter. Peter, Ming.

Peter: Nice to meet you, Ming…

Ming: Nice to meet you.

Peter: Are you from…

Ming: … from San Francisco—my parents are from Hong Kong, though.

Peter: Cool. I plan to spend my junior year in Hong Kong. Excuse me. Oh, that's my new roommate texting. He needs a key to the room. Sorry, I've got to go.

Jack: Wanna eat dinner with us first?

Peter: Nah, I can grab something later. Jack, where did you say you live?

Jack: Upstairs in Suite 33. Stop by sometime.

Peter: I will. Hope to see you, too, Ming.

Ming: Yeah, find me on Facebook. Ming Lee—L–E–E.

Peter: Okay. I will. Let's hang out sometime… Anyway, see you guys later. Have a nice dinner.

Jack: Thanks. Catch you later.

7 **Listening for Reductions** page 8

1. What did you do last weekend?
2. We've got to study tonight.
3. Jack, do you want to eat at the cafeteria?
4. I can meet you in half an hour.
5. Aren't you finished with the test yet?

9 **Distinguishing Among -s Endings** page 9

1. plays
2. misses
3. hopes
4. stops
5. drives
6. phones
7. washes
8. summarizes
9. mothers
10. puts

PART 2 Presentation: Freshman Workshop

3 **Listening for Main Ideas** page 13

4 **Listening for Specific Information** page 14

Lecturer: Good morning. We want to welcome all you new guys to this workshop on "Tips for Success" here at Faber College. I'm Terry Sargent, one of the counselors at Student Support Services.

Today we'll get started by talking about "time management," and later give you some ideas on good study skills.

Well… In high school, both your teachers and parents made sure you did your homework, got to school on time, and studied for your exams, right? They pretty much managed your schedule, your time. But in college, guess what: you're on your own. Students have a lot of freedom here, and that's not always easy to manage.

So here is tip number one: use a calendar or planner. Either online or off. Don't try to keep your schedule in your head. Write down your weekly schedule for everything: classes, social plans, exercise or sports, and appointments. For important things like deadlines or meetings, set your smart phone to remind you a day before, or an hour before.

Tip number two: make a to-do list every day. Write down all the things you plan to do that day, or put them in your cell phone. Start with the most important first. But don't put too many things on your list – keep your goals reasonable. When you finish something, cross it off your list. Before the day ends, try to start a new list for the next day.

And finally, tip number three: learn to say no. There are so many cool things to do on campus, so many new friends to hang out with—it's hard to stick to a schedule. But sometimes it's necessary to just say no and do what you planned.

Any questions so far? Sure?… OK, then, let's move on to the next topic.

PART 3 Strategies for Better Listening and Speaking

Focus on Testing: Using Context Clues page 15

Part 1

Peter: Wow, look at that line. Are you guys sure you want to wait?

Kenji: Uh, I'm hungry but I hate waiting. Is there another place that's not so crowded?

Ming: They're all crowded right now. It's lunchtime.

Question 1: Where are the students?

Peter: Okay. Let's eat here. At least this cafeteria has better food than the others on campus.

Part 2

Kenji: It took me over an hour to buy "Introduction to Economics" this morning.

Ming: Really? I just got mine online. It's so much easier.

Peter: Me, too. I just go to websites like Amazon or ecampus.com. They're cheaper, too.

Question 2: What do Ming and Peter buy online?

Kenji: Thanks for the tip. I already bought my textbooks for this term, but I'll buy them online next semester.

Part 3

Kenji: So what other tips do you have for me?

Peter: Do you work out?

Kenji: Yeah. Why?

Peter: Well, the gym gets super crowded in the evening. Not a good time to work out then.

Question 3: What is the meaning of "work out"?

Kenji: Oh, I see. But I like to exercise outside, not in the gym. I'm a runner.

Part 4

Ming: Oh, my mom is texting again. This is the fifth time today.

Peter: I know what you mean. My dad Skypes me whenever he knows I'm online.

Kenji: Oh, yeah. My mom sends these long emails, asking a thousand questions.

Question 4: What can you guess from this conversation?

Ming: When will they stop worrying about us so much?

Part 5

Peter: Speaking of worrying, I have a huge history test tomorrow. And a deadline for an English essay. I'm not going to get much sleep.

Ming: Hey, what about Jack's party tonight?

Peter: Oh, yeah. I forgot about that. I'll stop by for a little bit.

Question 5:
What can you guess about Peter?

Ming: Uh, Peter, I think you need to learn to manage your time better. Skip the party.

PART 4 Real-World Tasks: Using Voicemail Messages

1 Listening to Voicemail page 18

Example:

Outgoing Message: Your call has been forwarded to an automated voice messaging system. "Dave Mason" is not available. Record your message after the tone.

Jumi: Hi, Dave—this is Jumi from Math class. I'm still sick, so I'm going to need the homework assignment for Monday. If you have time, can you call me before 11 at 555-6639. You might have the number—that's my cell. Thanks a lot.

Message 1

Jon Gold: Hi, Peter. This is Jon Gold at Eagle Insurance getting back to you about your motorcycle. I think we can insure you for $122 a year, if you haven't had any accidents in the past three years. Call me— if I'm not here, you can talk to Bill at extension 3451.

Message 2

Kathy Jones: Hello, Ming. This is Kathy Jones. Sue Chen said you were looking for a part-time job. I might be able to offer you a little work at the bookstore. We need someone to help put out textbooks for next semester. If you can give me a call at 555-3000, extension 231, I'd like to schedule a brief interview with you sometime Friday.

Message 3

Dan: Yo, Joe, dude. I'm trying to reach your cousin Mary, but I can't find her number. She wants a ride from campus to our yoga class tomorrow afternoon. If you could let her know

to meet me around 4 at the entrance to campus parking lot A—that would be awesome.

Message 4

Steve: Hi, Kenji—it's Steve at State Street Wheels. Your bike's ready. To fix the frame was $35, and the seat we put on was an additional 27—the total's about $68 including tax. You can pick it up anytime today until 7:30.

Message 5

Jennifer: Hello—this message is for Dave Peterson. You left your cell phone at the library—anyway, don't worry—we'll hold it here for you at the information desk on the main floor. This is Jennifer, extension 5402, but any of the information librarians can get it for you. I'm putting it in a white envelope with your name on it. You'll need a photo ID to pick it up. And, uh, we'll be closing early, at 4, all next week for the break.

Message 6

Ellen: Hi, Ming—it's Ellen. I'm really sorry about this, but I had to change the restaurant for my roommate's party —the new restaurant is Korean—it's called Kim's Tofu House, and if you don't know it, it's on the corner of Telegraph and 23rd St. The reservation's still at 7 tonight—remember to get here by 6:45 so we're all inside to surprise her. See ya.

3 Calling for Information page 20

Ming: Hi, I'm calling about a parking permit.

Administrative Assistant:
Yes, you know you can get one online.

Ming: I know… but it wasn't clear from the website if parking lot nine is still available.

Admin: Yes, it is. I can take your information now to hold a space, if you like.

Ming: Great.

Admin: Your last name and student ID, please.

Ming: Lee—that's L as in Linda, E like Edward, E Edward. And my ID is K like Kangaroo, Y as in Yahoo, 6459.

Admin: KY6459? And you're Ming LEE?

Ming: Correct.

Admin: OK, I've got you on my screen… What's the year, make, and model of your car?

Ming: It's a 2010 Toyota Corolla.

Admin: License plate?

Ming: California plate AWJ one thirty.

Admin: AWJ one thirteen . . .

Ming: Sorry it's one, three, zero.

Admin: OK. That'll be $140 for the semester or $275 for the year.

Ming: Just for the semester. Can I pay today at Campus Parking Services?

Admin: That will be fine. Just be sure to pay and pick it up before tomorrow evening, all right?

Ming: Great—thanks for the help. Bye.

Admin: Bye.

CHAPTER **2** **Experiencing Nature**

Peter: Wow. Look. It's pouring again! I hate this weather. When does winter break start?

Jack: Winter break? It's only October.

Peter: I know, but I'm sick of studying. I want to go someplace warm and lie on the beach for a week. Someplace where it's sunny and dry. Florida or Hawaii, maybe?

Jack: Yeah. Where we can go swimming and snorkeling and get a great tan. Now that's my idea of a perfect vacation.

Ming: Not mine. I can't swim very well, and I don't like lying in the sun.

Peter: Oh, yeah? How come?

Ming: I don't know. I just prefer the mountains, especially in winter. I love snowboarding. In fact, I'm planning to go to Bear Mountain with some friends in December. Do you guys want to come?

Jack: No thanks. I went there last year. I was freezing the whole time. Anyway, I don't know how to ski very well. Last year I fell about a hundred times.

Ming: Peter, how about you?

Peter: Sorry, I'm like Jack. I don't want to go anyplace where it's below 70 degrees.

Jack: By the way, what's the weather forecast for tomorrow?

Ming: The same as today. Cloudy, cold, and a 90 percent chance of rain.

Jack: Oh, no! I left my umbrella at the library.

Ming: You can borrow mine. I've got an extra one.

Jack: Hi, Ming. Hi, Peter.

Ming and Peter: Hey, Jack.

Ming: What's happening?

Jack: I'm going to the campus recreation center. Do you want to come?

Ming: What are you going to do there?

Jack: Well, it's a nice day. We can swim and lie in the sun.

Ming: Thanks, but I don't want to go. I'm too tired.

Jack: How about you, Peter?

Peter: I can't. I've got to stay at home and study. Maybe tomorrow.

1. She can't swim very well.

2. Michael can drive.

3. The boys can cook.

4. I can't find his phone number.

5. Kenji can't speak Spanish.

6. He can speak Japanese.

7. I can't understand him.

8. Peter can come with us.

9. She can't take photographs in the rain.

10. Herb can play tennis very well.

PART 2   Story: Camping

(3) **Listening for Main Ideas** page 31

(4) **Taking Notes on Specific Information** page 31

Manager: You're all wet and muddy. What happened to you?

Woman: You're not going to believe this! It's the most incredible thing! It all started when we decided to go hiking this morning.

Man: Yeah, the weather was sunny and clear when we got up. So we put on shorts and T-shirts and went hiking. Half an hour later it started pouring!

Woman: So we hiked back to our tent as fast as we could. We couldn't wait to change into dry clothes.

Man: Right. But when we went into our tent, we couldn't find our clothes! So we went back outside to look around. And then we saw the craziest thing. Two great big brown bears came out of the woods, and guess what? They were wearing our clothes!

Manager: Aw, come on. That's impossible! What do you mean, the bears were wearing your clothes?

Man: Well, one bear had my T-shirt around his neck. And the other one had Mary's pants over his head. We still don't know where the rest of our clothes are!

Manager: [laughing]

Woman: I know it sounds funny, but we were so scared! Those bears

were big! And now we have a big problem.

Manager: What's that?

Woman and Man: We don't have any dry clothes to wear!

PART 3   Strategies for Better Listening and Speaking

Focus on Testing: Using Context Clues page 35

Conversation 1

A: Nice weather we're having.

B: Yes. Isn't it a nice surprise? At this time it's usually much cooler and raining already.

A: Well, this weather will probably end soon; all the leaves on the trees are brown, and the nights are getting cold.

Conversation 2

A: Take your coat; it's freezing outside.

B: Nah, I'm only going to the corner store. I'll be back in five minutes.

A: I'm telling you, it's in the low thirties out there. Do you want to get sick?

Conversation 3

A: How do you like all this rain?

B: Well, it's good for the trees and flowers.

A: Yes, it's nice to see the leaves coming back on the trees again.

B: Yeah, and I'm glad the snow is all gone.

Conversation 4

A: Is it hot enough for you?

B: Whew… it sure is. I don't mind the heat so much. It's the humidity that bothers me. Look, I'm all wet.

A: Me too. Let's go get a cold drink somewhere.

B: Yeah, someplace with air conditioning.

Conversation 5

A: Ah, this is the life. No traffic, no worries. Just lie here and enjoy doing nothing.

B: Honey, your back is turning red. If you're not careful, you're going to get sunburned.

A: Could you put some sun screen on my back?

Conversation 1

A: What's the weather like today?

B: Hot and humid and about ninety-five degrees.

Conversation 2

A: I'm going to take a swim. Want to come?

B: Is the pool heated?

A: Sure. It's probably over eighty degrees.

Conversation 3

A: How was your skiing holiday?

B: Great! The weather was in the thirties and we had perfect snow conditions.

Conversation 4

A: Let's go for a walk.

B: What's it like out?

A: About forty degrees, but the wind has stopped.

B: Thanks, but I think I'll stay inside where it's warm.

Conversation 5

A: It's a hundred and three in here! Why don't you turn on the air conditioning?

B: It's broken.

Conversation 6

A: How was the weather in Europe this summer?

B: Just lovely. Hot, but never over thirty degrees.

A: Thirty? Oh, you mean Celsius.

Conversation 7

A: What's wrong?

B: It's thirteen below outside and I can't find my gloves.

A: Here. Use mine. I have an extra pair.

Conversation 8

A: Did you check the weather forecast?

B: Yeah. It's supposed to be in the high seventies this weekend.

A: The seventies? I guess we can forget about skiing.

Female voice: This is the National Weather Service report at five in the afternoon, Friday. The forecast for the Bear Mountain area is partly cloudy with some showers through the night, clearing by early morning. The high today was sixty-one degrees; overnight lows will be in the mid-fifties. Tomorrow's highs will be in the sixties with fair skies continuing throughout the day. Temperatures will drop Saturday night to a chilly low of forty-five degrees. Sunday will continue fair, warming up to a high temperature of seventy degrees. Sunday night lows will get down below fifty again. There will be a fifty percent chance of rain on Monday.

CHAPTER 3 Living to Eat, or Eating to Live?

Andrew: Well, I got a few groceries that aren't on the list.

Nancy: I can see that! We're not shopping for an army, you know.

Andrew: I always do this when I'm hungry.

Nancy: Well, let's see what you have here.

Andrew: Some nice, fresh strawberries for only $1.79 a pound.

Nancy: Well, that's fine. They always have nice produce here. But why do you have all these cookies?

Andrew: Don't you like them?

Nancy: Oh, I don't know… I hope you got a box of tofu.

Andrew: I think I forgot. Where's the aisle with the Asian foods again?

Nancy: Aisle three.

Andrew: I'll go get it.

Nancy: Wait—this steak you got looks really expensive!

Andrew: Well, it isn't. It's on sale for just $3.99 a pound.

Nancy: And what's this? More ice cream? We already have a quart at home. Why don't you put it back? Meanwhile, I'll get in line right here.

Cashier: I'm sorry, Miss; this is the express line, and it looks like you've got more than ten items. Oh, and we don't take checks here.

7 **Listening for Reductions** page 45

Customer: Waiter?

Server: Yes, sir. Do you know what you want?

Customer: Do you have the spaghetti with mushroom sauce tonight?

Server: Yes, we do.

Customer: Well, are the mushrooms fresh or canned?

Server: They're fresh, and the sauce has lots of them.

Customer: Great, I'll have that.

Server: Do you want something to drink?

Customer: I don't know. Why don't you recommend something?

Server: How about some nice Italian mineral water?

9 **Distinguishing between Teens and Tens** page 46

1. We waited in line for 30 minutes.
2. My sister is 14 years old.
3. We've lived in this city for 15 years.
4. Sixty people came to the party.
5. The groceries cost 70 dollars.

6. There are 18 students in the class.
7. I live 90 miles from my parents.

10 **Listening for Teens and Tens** page 47

1. This turkey weighs 14 pounds.
2. The market is open until 10:30.
3. We spent $40 on groceries yesterday.
4. This milk is good until November 13th.
5. Those peaches cost $1.90 a pound.
6. Everything in this store is about 15 percent cheaper today.
7. I'm having a big party this weekend. I need 30 bottles of mineral water.
8. The store will close in 15 minutes.
9. By using this coupon, you can save 70 cents on this ice cream.
10. Canned vegetables are in Aisle 19.

PART 2 Advice Show: Healthy Eating

3 **Listening for Main Ideas** page 50

4 **Taking Notes on Specific Information** page 50

Bob: Hi everyone, I'm Bob.

Pam: And I'm Pam, and this show is all about "Eating Right!"

Bob: You know, Pam, with people so busy today, they don't have a lot of time to shop or plan what to eat.

Pam: That's true, but healthy eating might just give you a longer and happier life! So here are some things we all should think about regarding our diet.

Bob: First, eat lots of fruits and vegetables. Why? Well, they're a good source of vitamins and minerals….

Pam: Right, and they're a good source of fiber, too. Also, they're almost all low in calories and fat, and eating them may help protect you against cancer. So, put an apple or a banana in your lunchbox, or have a carrot for a snack—skip those potato chips.

Bob: That's right. Fruits make a great dessert—you don't need all those sugary sweets and drinks, cookies, cakes, candies, sodas.

Pam: You bet you don't. So a second point to remember: too much sugar in your diet can lead to health problems like weight gain, tooth decay—that's trips to your dentist…

Bob: Owww! Or even diabetes, and that's serious!

Pam: Now the third thing we want you to think about is reducing the fat you eat.

Bob: Uh-huh. Cutting down on the fat in our diets would be good for many of us.

Pam: So true. It can help us lose weight.

Bob: Or *not* gain weight in the first place.

Pam: And it can lower our chance of getting heart disease, and cancer, too.

Bob: So cut back on all those hamburgers, cheeseburgers, French fries…

Pam: And chips—they're full of fat…

Bob: And salt. Oh, I don't want to forget our fourth suggestion: eat more whole grains. You'll get plenty of fiber, vitamins, and minerals from them.

Pam: You mean, like, brown rice and whole wheat?

Bob: That's it. They're much healthier than white bread, white rice, and things like that.

Pam: Finally, you don't want to drink too much coffee. Coffee can make you nervous, and keep you awake at night. Or even affect your heart—but we'll talk about coffee on another show.

PART 3 Strategies for Better Listening and Speaking

Focus on Testing: Using Context Clues page 53

Conversation 1

Server: Good evening. My name is Pierre. Would you like something to drink?

Bob: No, thanks. But we would like to order some appetizers.

Server: Certainly, here are your menus. Our specials tonight are lemon chicken and fresh broiled swordfish.

Question 1: *The speakers are in a…*

Susan: This is such a beautiful restaurant, Bob. Thanks for bringing me here.

Conversation 2

Felipe: Why don't we sit at the counter? There aren't any free tables.

Salim: Fine.

Waitress: Coffee?

Felipe: Yes.

Salim: Yes, please.

Waitress: I'll be right back to take your order.

Question 2: *The speakers are in a…*

Felipe: This is my favorite diner. The prices are low and the service is great.

Conversation 3

A: These salads look great. Do you want one?

B: No, I want a hot dish from over there.

Server: Yes, what would you like?

A: Is that mushroom soup?

Server: No, it's bean soup.

A: How much is it?

Server: It's two dollars a bowl. You pay down there at the cashier.

Question 3: *The speakers are in a…*

B: I hear this cafeteria is open all night.

Conversation 4

Server: May I take your order?

John: I'll have two burritos, no onions, and two small Cokes.

Server: For here or to go?

John: For here. Oh, and an order of nachos.

Server: That'll be eight dollars.

Question 4: *The speakers are in a....*

John: I know fast food is fattening, but I really love it.

PART 4 Real-World Tasks: Recipes and Regional Foods

② Taking Notes on a Recipe page 56

Tom: To make French toast for four people, here's what you'll need: eight slices of bread, two eggs, one cup of milk, one-half teaspoon of salt, and about a tablespoon of butter. Have you got all that?

First, beat the eggs, milk, and salt with a fork for a minute until they're well mixed.

Then melt the butter in a frying pan. While the butter is melting, dip eight slices of bread into the egg mixture.

Then, when the butter is hot, fry the bread slices until they're golden brown.

Serve them on a warm plate with butter and syrup or jam.

⑥ Regional Foods page 59

Paula: Vancouver, in Western Canada, has delicious Chinese food because there are many Chinese immigrants in that part of Canada. And Vancouver has great fish—like salmon.

San Francisco also has excellent Chinese and Japanese restaurants. Oh and the bread in San Francisco is really special. Just north of San Francisco, there are two little towns called Napa and Sonoma. That's where they make some wonderful California wine.

Now, if you drive to Texas, be sure to eat some Mexican food. It's very spicy, but so delicious. In the Midwest, the middle of the United States, you can find terrific cheese in Wisconsin. And don't forget to have a steak in Chicago. The beef is very good there.

If you drive to the Northeast, try to visit Maine to taste the seafood. Lobster is fantastic. And nearby, in Montreal, Canada, the French food is fabulous. Oh, and if you decide to go down south to Georgia, fried chicken is very popular. And in Florida, of course, you'll find the best oranges.

CHAPTER 4 In the Community

PART 1 Conversation: Getting Out into the Community

③ Listening for Main Ideas page 66

④ Listening for Details page 66

⑤ Listening for Stressed Words page 66

Peter: Dude, you still have the computer on? You've been here on Facebook and Skype for hours!

Kenji: I'm just chatting with some friends. I guess I lost track of time.

Peter: Yeah, you're online way too much. You've got to get out more. It'll help your English.

Kenji: To tell you the truth, I'm not sure where to go. I'm still kind of new here. And I have to study!

Peter: Well, there is tons of stuff to do in town.

Kenji: Like what?

Peter: Like the free concert in the park last Saturday, and…

Kenji: Oh. I watched some of it on YouTube.

Peter: See what I mean? You're not going to meet anyone that way! Come hang out with us more.

Kenji: OK, what are you guys doing this weekend?

Peter: There is this street festival downtown. It's supposed to have some great ethnic food, some bands, and an art show. We're going to ride our bikes there.

Kenji: Sounds good. Saturday or Sunday?

Peter: Actually, it's both days. But we're going to go on Saturday because Sunday we're doing community service.

Kenji: Community service? You mean like volunteering?

Peter: Yeah. That's another thing you should do with us. We volunteer at a homeless shelter twice a month. It's really cool because we get to help out and meet some interesting people at the same time.

Kenji: Hmm... I might be interested in that. Can I just show up?

Peter: Yeah, I guess so, but first sign up online. The link is www.volunteer .com. Just don't stay on the Internet forever...

Kenji: Man, you sound just like my mother. OK, I'll study a bit more, then look up that link.

7 **Listening for Reductions** page 68

A: So I hear you're going to study in the U.S.— in Los Angeles, right?

B: Yeah. I'm excited! There's tons of stuff to do there. You have got to come visit me.

A: O.K. I'll just show up at your door one day and surprise you.

B: Great... Oh wow it's late. Let's get out of here. We're supposed to meet Anshu for dinner in ten minutes.

A: Sorry I got here late—I kind of lost track of time.

B: No problem. We can catch a taxi.

PART 2 Conversation: Choosing a College Location

3 **Listening for Main Ideas** page 73

4 **Taking Notes on Specific Information** page 74

A: So, Jessie, you picked this school because of the business department, right? I mean the academics...

Jessie: Yeah, mostly because of its academic reputation. But that's not the only reason.

A: Oh?

Jessie: I also liked the community the college is in. I'm from a small town, and I was really excited about living in a big city like this; in an urban environment. If you choose a college in a small town, you spend most of your time on campus. You get to know your classmates and your dorm mates really well, and that's good, but there is not much to do outside campus. I wanted something bigger.

A: How is this community different from your home town?

Jessie: Oh, it's a lot more diverse. I mean, in my home town there was no variety, everyone knew each other, everyone was from the same background. Here, my neighbors are from around the world, there're lots of ethnic restaurants, lots of cool jazz clubs, always tons of stuff do. And it's easy to get to great museums, parks, and stuff like that. I take the subway everywhere—it's so convenient.

A: So the campus is right in the center of the city?

Jessie: Oh, yeah. Everything I need is nearby: laundromat, great coffee shops with wifi where I can study, there's a little store around the corner that's open 24 hours, you know, if I need to get basic groceries.

A: So what's the downside?

Jessie: The downside? Well, there is so much to do in this city, it can be distracting. You know what I mean? A young 18-year-old can get very excited and want to do everything and see everything, go out late at night... you know, it's hard to focus on your studies.

A: Did that happen to you?

Jessie: Yeah, a little bit. My grades were not great freshman year. But I've learned to balance things—do my school work and also enjoy this great community.

PART 3 Strategies for Better Listening and Speaking

Focus on Testing: Using Context Clues page 75

Conversation 1

A: We need to go downtown. Which track is that?

B: Track 4. You need to go downstairs. See that sign? "Eastbound." You wanna go east.

A: Oh, no, we just missed it.

B: That's okay. All the cars were full anyway. We can catch the express in about 5 minutes.

Question 1: *Where are the speakers?*

A: This is the most crowded subway station I've ever seen.

Conversation 2

A: I really need to wake up. Do they give free refills here?

B: I dunno. I think you pay for each cup.

A: Oh! My iPad just found a signal. Check your email?

B: Sure—just let me find some cream and sugar.

Question 2: *Where are the speakers?*

A: I think the wi-fi in this coffee shop is better than Starbucks'.

Conversation 3

A: Wow, it's so crowded!

B: Sure… Everyone loves all this fresh, organic stuff.

A: Look at those beautiful veggies.

B: Yeah, I know. You won't find tomatoes like that at the supermarket.

A: Well, you're buying everything directly from the people who grow it.

Question 3: *Where are the speakers?*

B: Too bad the farmers' market is only open on Saturdays.

Conversation 4

A: Oh, no. All the machines are taken.

B: Wait. That one is almost done. Go ahead, take that one. You only have one load.

A: Thanks. Let me get some detergent and some change. It's $2.50 a load, right?

B: Right. And $3.50 for the dryer.

Question 4: *Where are the speakers?*

B: Wow. Let's find a cheaper laundromat next time.

Conversation 5

Man: I just need a trim, mostly in the back.

Woman: So you don't want me to cut the front at all?

Man: Just a little, so it doesn't get in my eyes.

Woman: All right. Let's get you shampooed.

Man: OK. Let me go take my jacket off.

Question 5: *Who is the man talking to?*

Man: It's so quiet here today. Where are the other hairstylists?

PART 4 Real-World Tasks: Asking for and Giving Directions

② Following Directions page 79

Conversation 1

A: Jessie, where is the nearest supermarket?

Jessie: Oh, there is Ralph's just down the street on Le Conte. But I prefer Whole Foods.

A: Oh, I've heard of Whole Foods. Is that far from here?

Jessie: No, not really. Just walk down Westwood, one block. Turn right on Weyburn, go two blocks, and make a left on Gayley. Whole Foods is in the middle of the block.

A: So one block on Westwood, two blocks on Weyburn?

Jessie: Right. It's pretty easy to find.

Conversation 2

B: I need to get some cash. Is there an ATM nearby?

Jessie: An ATM? Let's see. There is a Citi Bank a couple of blocks from here. Go west on Le Conte, and make a left on Broxton. You'll see a cookie shop, Diddy Riese Cookies, on your left. Citi Bank is right across the street.

Conversation 3

C: How can I get to a drugstore? I heard there's a CVS on Glendon.

Jessie: Yes, there is one on Glendon. Between Weyburn and Kinross.

C: Do I go north?

Jessie: No, go south, south on Westwood and make a left on Weyburn. Turn right on Glendon. Go past Trader Joe's; you'll see the CVS on the other side, in the middle of the block.

C: Wait, so I go south on Glendon and the CVS will be on my right?

Jessie: Yes, exactly.

Conversation 4

D: We're looking for a good place to eat Thai food. Do you know any?

Jessie: Thai food? Do you want to walk or are you driving?

D: We want something nearby. Walking distance.

Jessie: OK. Let me Google it… Oh, here is one: Thai Café. It got pretty good reviews.

D: Is it nearby?

Jessie: Yeah, on Tiverton. Go down one block to Weyburn. Turn left and walk two blocks until you see Tiverton. Make a right and walk one block, almost to the corner. The Thai Café is on the west side, across from Denny's.

3 Getting Directions page 80

Conversation 1

A: Hotel concierge. May I help you?

B: Hi, I'm in Room 318. I need to get to the new Apple Store. Can I walk there?

A: It's easier to catch the Number 8 bus—it goes right there, and it runs every five minutes.

B: OK, then where can I catch it—and, sorry, what's the fare?

A: There's a stop right across the street from the hotel. Going west. And it's a dollar seventy-five.

B: Thanks—and then where do I get off?

A: At the corner of University and Pine.

Then walk back one block on University to Bush Street. You'll see the Apple sign on the right.

B: Well that sounds pretty easy…

A: It is—just make sure you get on the 8, not an 8A, or 8B—they won't get you where you want to go.

Conversation 2

A: Hi—can we help you with that map?

B: Actually, yeah… thanks—do you know how to get to Saint Mark's Place?

A: Well, the subway is fastest. You can go downstairs right here to the station and get on the Number 7 train east.

B: So the 7 takes me to Saint Mark's…

A: No, you'll get off at the Lexington Avenue station and change to a Number 6, south.

B: So the 7 to the 6…

A: Right, then get off at Astor Place—about four stops. Go upstairs and ask anyone—Saint Mark's is right there.

B: Astor Place—got it—well, thanks a lot!

A: No problem.

Conversation 3

A: Hi, Mark! My plane just landed—I'm here!

B: Great. I'm sorry I couldn't pick you up—uh, the train to Berkeley isn't too bad.

A: No problem—just tell me what to do.

B: Well, look for a sign for the Air Train station. Which terminal are you at?

A: International terminal G.

B: OK, well from G, get on the Air Train Blue line—*not* red, and go one stop to Garage G. When you get off, look for the arrow to the San Francisco train. It's called "BART"—that's B, A, R, T.

A: So get off at "G" like George, and change to a BART train?

B: Correct. Get a ticket to Berkeley from a machine. It's about $9.

A: OK, then which train?

B: Go to the San Francisco track—that's north, and make sure you get on a train to

Richmond—that's the only one that goes to Berkeley.

A: So, Air Train, Blue line, to BART, then a Richmond train, north?

B: Perfect. I'll be at the Berkeley station— you'll arrive in a little over an hour. See you soon.

A: See you.

PART 1 Conversation: Renting an Apartment

3 **Listening for Main Ideas** page 85

4 **Listening for Details** page 86

5 **Listening for Stressed Words** page 86

Mgr: Hello?

Olivia: Hi. My name is Olivia. I'm calling about the apartment for rent.

Mgr: Oh, yes. Which one?

Olivia: The two bedroom one bath for $1,150

Mgr: OK. That one is still available.

Olivia: I see. It's unfurnished, right?

Mgr: Right.

Olivia: Can you tell me a little more about it? Like, uh, where is it exactly?

Mgr: We're at National Boulevard and Bundy. Did you see our ad online?

Olivia: Yes, on Craigslist. It says you're near bus lines—that's good, 'cause I go to school every day.

Mgr: Oh, so you're a college student. How many people is this for?

Olivia: Just me and my roommate. Um, can you tell me, is there laundry on-site?

Mgr: Yes, there's on-site laundry, just not in the unit though. We have a laundry room downstairs. It's a very nice

building, security entrance, elevator, you've got a nice view of the park…

Olivia: That's good. What kind of deposit do you require?

Mgr: Well, I can email you an application; it explains everything. But the main thing we require is one-month rent as a security deposit and a $200 cleaning fee—that's not refundable. And of course we require a credit check.

Olivia: Oh, I see. Well, my roommate and I are international students, so I'm not sure about the credit…

Mgr: Well, you know what? Don't worry about that right now. Why don't you come by and see the place. I'm here 9 to 5 every day.

Olivia: OK, we can come by later today, around 4:30. Can you give me the exact address?

Mgr: 5443 National. And your name was Olivia, right?

Olivia: Right. Olivia Sandoval. Are you the landlord?

Mgr: No, I'm the manager. I'm Larry. My office is next to the front door.

Olivia: OK. I'll see you later then.

Mgr: See you later. Bye.

7 **Listening for Reductions** page 88

Steve: Uh-oh. I can't find my keys.

Margot: What kind of keys? House keys?

Steve: Yeah.

Margot: Don't you have an extra one?

Steve: Yeah, but not with me. I gave an extra key to one of the neighbors.

Margot: OK, then you can get your keys from him.

Steve: No, 'cause he's on vacation.

Margot: Then you're going to need to call a locksmith.

Steve: OK, give me your phone.

Margot: Why? Did you lose your phone too?

Steve: No, it's locked in the house.

9 **Distinguishing Among** *–ed*
Endings page 89

1. turned		6.	walked
2. rented		7.	tested
3. mixed		8.	followed
4. asked		9.	moved
5. recommended		10.	changed

PART 2   Presentation: Student Housing Choices

3 **Listening for Main Ideas** page 93

4 **Taking Notes on Specific Information** page 93

Eddie: Hi, guys, I'm Eddie, here in student housing. I know there's a lot to think about before starting college... like, "where am I gonna live?" Well, let's look at some choices, and their pros and cons. If you have questions, please jump in.

So first let's compare campus dorms—that's dormitories, with the university co-op— I'll explain what a co-op is in a minute. Afterwards, I can answer questions about off-campus apartments, or homestays if we have time.

OK. As you may know, we've got excellent dorms right here on campus. Now, the dorms are not as cheap as off-campus housing, but we think you get a lot of value. You can get to all your classes in five minutes or so. In most dorms, students share bedrooms with one roommate, but if you really want privacy, you can usually find a single.

Student Q: Do they have kitchens—I mean, can we cook for ourselves?

Eddie: Not in the older dorms—you'll have to sign up for a plan, and eat all your meals in one of the dining halls or cafés.

Our two new dorms are different, though: on every floor, in each wing, we have four bedrooms grouped together to share a living room, a kitchen, and a bathroom. So in the new dorms, you *can* cook, but you'll still have to buy a meal plan.

3 Students:
Really? Oh. Jeez.

Eddie: Well... Another nice thing about the dorms is, since they're on campus, they're patrolled by the university police. I'm happy to say, we don't have a problem with stealing or violence on campus—off-campus might be a little different.

Now, have any of you heard of a co-op? Well "co-op" stands for a "cooperative"—a group that works together.

The co-op kind of looks like a dorm, but students who live there actually manage their own building. Also, the residents have to agree to do four hours of work a week—stuff like cleaning, food shopping, or cooking.

Costs are really low; much less than in a dorm. A friend of mine loves it—she's met great, open-minded friends and she says it's a good way to practice your English if you're an international student.

The co-op here in town is about a 10-minute walk from campus—not bad if the weather's good. The downside is, rooms in the co-op are pretty small, and right now, only triple rooms are available—no doubles or singles. So there's not much privacy, right?

Student Q: What about bathrooms?

Eddie: They're shared. Residents of a hallway use common bathrooms.

Also, in the co-op the furniture and decorating is kind of "informal"—you know, it's kind of...

Student Q: You mean it's a mess?

Eddie: Not at all—the co-op's just not updated as frequently as the dorms are. To be fair, some students find the dorm interiors a little cold and boring. If you're interested, we can arrange visits to the co-op and several dorms.

So now let's briefly look at some of the other choices...

PART 3 Strategies for Better Listening and Speaking

Focus on Testing: Using Context Clues page 95

Conversation 1

Ali: Property Management, Ali speaking.

Judy: Hi, Ali. This is Judy from unit 206. Just wanna tell you, my place is still incredibly hot.

Ali: Still? Didn't the repairman come on Monday?

Judy: He did, but he didn't fix it right, I guess. It's 35 degrees in my apartment even though I set the temperature on 20. So now I have to keep all my windows open.

Question 1:
What is broken in Judy's apartment?

Ali: OK. I'll send another air conditioning repairman tomorrow.

Conversation 2

Woman: My rent is so high; I just can't continue living here.

Man: So why don't you move?

Woman: I want to but I have a one-year lease.

Man: What happens if you break the lease?

Woman: I'll have to pay the rent for one year even if I move.

Man: Hmm. How about getting a roommate to share the rent?

Question 2:
What can you guess about the situation?

Man: I know you like living alone, but having a roommate will save you money.

Conversation 3

Woman 1: Chris, can I talk to you about something?

Woman 2: Yeah. What's up?

Woman 1: I'm really uncomfortable about your friend staying over so often.

Woman 2: Kim? Why? Don't you like her?

Woman 1: No, that's not it. It's just that she is here all the time, and this is a small place and...

Woman 2: ... but when we moved in together, we agreed that we can have friends over.

Woman 1: Yes, but not so often. And not overnight! I find Kim on the living room couch almost every morning.

Question 3: *Who are the speakers?*

Woman 2: Well, you've been a good roommate, so I don't want to cause any problems. I won't ask Kim to come over so often.

Conversation 4

Man: Yes?

Woman: Hi. I'm Tonya. I live next door. Um, did you get my note?

Man: Hmm. What note?

Woman: I wrote you a note about your music the other day.

Man: What's wrong with my music?

Woman: Well, you know it's 11:30 and I really need to go to sleep.

Man: Um, I'm just, you know, having a little party with some friends.

Woman: I understand, but two days ago it was the same thing. I couldn't sleep half the night!

Question 4: *What is the problem?*

Man: Hey, no problem. I didn't realize it was too loud. I'll turn it down, OK?

Conversation 5

Woman: This will be your room. You see the bathroom is right here next door.

Man: So it's my private bath, right?

Woman: Right. And there is the kitchen. We all like to cook and you're welcome to use it too.

Man:	Great. Can I see the backyard?
Woman:	Sure. It's right this way. It's huge and very quiet because there are no neighbors on the other side.

Question 5:
What type of housing is the woman showing?

Man:	Wow. The backyard is the best part of the house. I think I'll like it here.

PART 4 Real-World Tasks: Home Exchange: Taking Care of Someone's House

1 Arranging a "Home Exchange" page 96

Mary:	So, Dave—before I head to the airport, let's just go over the things on this list—just a few rules, like… please don't eat outside the kitchen or dining room.
Dave:	Of course.
Mary:	You can use the desktop computer and all the video stuff—just don't leave anything on overnight…
Dave:	Right…
Mary:	No fires in the fireplace—a visitor actually burned down my friend's place.
Dave:	You're kidding!
Mary:	And um, no parties or overnight guests… sorry…
Dave:	Yes ma'am…
Mary:	Come on… oh and please don't use those porcelain coffee cups. It's an expensive collection. OK… now the things I need done are pretty simple, and they're on the list: water the plants once or twice a week, put your garbage out front in the brown container, Tuesday morning by 8, and finally, collect the mail and the newspaper every day. When you're done with the newspapers give them to Mrs. Cervantes—the neighbor to the left side—she uses them in her garden, I think.

Dave:	And where's the mail again?
Mary:	It falls on the floor inside the front door—just put it all in a bag in my little office. That's it, I think. So, as far as your place goes, I remember it pretty well… but remind me.
Dave:	Yeah, pretty simple—it's a small apartment, right? So remember, shoes off in the apartment—
Mary:	I know: new carpets and all…
Dave:	Right… and don't leave *any* food unwrapped for a minute, even in the kitchen—bugs find it fast… And… no loud music after 10 P.M.—neighbors will complain… that's all…
Mary:	Ah yes, apartment living… and what did you want me to take care of?
Dave:	Oh, you can get my mail, too… the mailbox is in the lobby—here's an extra key. My mail goes in the green box under my bed. Oh and my cleaning person, Eva, comes on Wednesdays at 11 A.M. She has a key—but can you remember to leave her $40 cash on the dining table?
Mary:	Sure.
Dave:	So when you leave NY at the end of the month, just leave the keys on the kitchen counter and make sure the front door is locked when you pull it shut.
Mary:	I will. Listen, it's getting pretty late—I gotta get to the airport—just text or Skype me about anything we missed…
Dave:	OK. You want me to drive you to the airport?
Mary:	You drive my Audi? No way… I'll get a cab…

2 Listening to Instructions on Where to Put Furniture page 97

Frederick:	Thanks for helping me redecorate. So where should I put everything?
Cynthia:	Well, let's start with that giant TV—put it up on the left short wall, OK?

Frederick: Fine.

Cynthia: Then the sofa, of course, should face the TV—I'd say from the right edge of your rug.

Frederick: That makes sense.

Cynthia: Put the coffee table in front of the sofa, and the floor lamp on the side of the sofa away from the windows—you can use a little extra light there.

Frederick: That's what I was thinking.

Cynthia: And then the little end table goes on the other side of the sofa. You might want to buy a nice small table lamp to put on it...

Frederick: OK—where's the best spot for the easy chair?

Cynthia: Facing the window along the lower edge of the rug not too far from the floor lamp.

Frederick: So someone sitting in it can chat with someone on the sofa, watch TV, or enjoy the view out the window. Perfect.

Cynthia: Well, try it out for a while—we can always rethink it if it doesn't work for you.

CHAPTER **6** **Cultures of the World**

PART 1 Conversation: Learning New Customs

Kenji: So, Salma, is this your first trip to the United States?

Salma: Yes, it is.

Kenji: And what's your impression so far?

Salma: Well, the people are really friendly, and the city is beautiful. But the food; well, it's not so good.

Kenji: Oh, yeah, that's what I thought too when I first got here. But I'm used to American food now. I actually love hot dogs and French fries.

Yolanda: So last night I took Salma to a Mexican restaurant. I wanted her to try something exotic.

Kenji: Did you like it?

Salma: Yeah, the food was pretty good, but it was too much. I couldn't finish it all.

Yolanda: Salma was amazed when I took the leftovers home in a doggie bag.

Kenji: Yeah, that's funny, isn't it? They call it a doggie bag but it's for people. Anyway, what else surprised you?

Salma: That the restaurant was so cold! We don't use air conditioning so much in my country. Oh, and the water had ice in it, too. I had to put on my sweater, I was so cold!

Salma: Excuse me. Hello? Oh, hi, Eduardo.

Waitress: Excuse me Miss, but we don't allow cell phones in the restaurant.

Salma: Oh, sorry. I didn't know... Eduardo, I'll have to call you back... That's strange for me. In Lebanon we use phones *everywhere*. I mean, we try to talk quietly in a place like this, but...

Kenji: Same in Japan. This kind of rule is getting more popular, though.

Yolanda: I'm sorry, Salma.

Salma: No, no, it's OK. When in Rome, do as the Romans do.

Anita: Well, it's time to get back to the office. I'll see you soon, Brenda.

Brenda: OK, see you... Wait, Anita, is this your cell phone?

Anita: Oh my goodness, yes, thanks. By the way, I almost forgot: my parents are coming for a visit next week.

Brenda: Really? I'd love to meet them.

Anita: Well, do you want to have lunch with us on Saturday?

Brenda: Saturday? Hmm... I promised my roommate I would go shopping with her that day. Could we get together for coffee later in the afternoon?

Anita: I don't know. They might be busy, but I'll ask.

PART 2   Lecture: Coming-of-Age Ceremonies

3 Listening for Main Ideas page 108

4 Taking Notes on Specific Information page 109

Lecturer: At what age does a child become an adult? The answer depends on your culture or religion. Here are a few examples.

First, in some North American Indian cultures, a boy becomes a man around the age of 13. At that time, he goes into the woods alone, without food or water, for several days. When he returns safely, he becomes an adult man. Girls become adult women as soon as they are old enough to have babies, also around the age of 12 or 13.

In the Jewish religion, children spend years studying their history and religion. Then, at age 13 for boys and 12 for girls, they go through an important religious ceremony. The boys' ceremony is called a bar mitzvah and the girls' is called a bat mitzvah. From that day, they are adults, and they are responsible for their own religious development.

In Japan today, young people become legal adults at age 20. Each year on the second Monday in January, they celebrate "Coming-of-Age Day," when all the twenty-year-olds in a town are invited to attend a special ceremony. They wear traditional clothes, listen to speeches, and visit with old friends.

Finally, in the United States, the passage into adulthood takes several years. American teenagers look forward to their 16th birthday, because in most states that is the age when they can get a driver's license. The legal age of adulthood is 18, when Americans can vote, get married, and work full-time.

PART 3   Strategies for Better Listening and Speaking

Focus on Testing: Using Context Clues page 112

Conversation 1

Yuka: Hi, Belinda.

Belinda: Hi, Yuka. What are you doing here?

Yuka: Oh, I was in your neighborhood. I just wanted to say hi.

Belinda: Uh, that's nice. Uh...

Yuka: Are you busy?

Belinda: Uh, yes, a little bit. But come in for a few minutes, anyway.

Question 1: *What mistake did Yuka make?*

Yuka: I'm sorry I didn't call before I came. I'll only stay a few minutes.

Conversation 2

Customer: Excuse me, waiter!

Waiter: Yes, are you ready to pay, sir?

Customer: Yes, here you are.

Waiter: Thank you. Uh... Excuse me, sir. Was there a problem with your food?

Customer: No. It was delicious, thank you.

Waiter: Uh, was the service OK? I mean, did I do anything...?

Customer: No, you were great. Excellent service.

Waiter: Oh, OK. I just, uh, wasn't sure...

Question 2:
What mistake did the customer probably make?

Customer: Oh, I almost forgot. Here's your tip.

Conversation 3

Woman: So how was your neighbor's party last night?

Man: Fine, but the beginning was kind of strange.

Woman: Oh? What happened?

Man: My neighbor said the party started at 8 o'clock. So I went there at exactly 8:00. I couldn't believe it: she was still in the shower, the food wasn't ready, and there were no guests.

Woman: So what did you do?

Man: Oh, I just sat down and waited for about half an hour. Then people began to arrive and the party got started.

Question 3: Who made a mistake?

Woman: I guess you didn't know: in the U.S., people never arrive at parties exactly on time.

Conversation 4

Man: Wow, this is a great house!

Woman: Thanks.

Man: When did you move in?

Woman: We bought it two months ago. We finally moved in last week.

Man: How much did you pay for it?

Woman: Uh, well, it was a good, I mean, uh, a pretty good price, uh... Would you like a drink or something?

Man: Yeah, a glass of water would be great, thanks.

Question 4: What mistake did the man make?

Man: It was rude of me to ask how much you paid. I'm sorry.

Conversation 5

Woman: I don't understand my new neighbors from Korea.

Man: What do you mean?

Woman: Well, yesterday was my neighbor Hyun-Ee's birthday. So I told her happy birthday and put my arms around her. You know, to give her a big hug.

Man: Uh-oh. What did she do?

Woman: She looked uncomfortable and kind of pushed me away. Don't you think that's rude?

Man: No. She probably thought *you* were rude.

Question 5:
What didn't the American woman know?

Man: In Korea, it's not customary to hug people you don't know very well.

PART 4 Real-World Tasks: Dining Customs

3 **Following Directions for Setting a Table** page 116

Mrs. Riley: OK, so we start by putting the napkin in the center of the dinner plate, like this.

Ming: All right. Now what?

Mrs. Riley: Well, let's put the glasses out. Are you planning to serve wine?

Ming: Yes, of course.

Mrs. Riley: White or red?

Ming: Uh... does it matter?

Mrs. Riley: Well, there are different glasses for each kind of wine.

Ming: I see. Well, I plan to serve roast beef.

Mrs. Riley: In that case you'll need these glasses here. They're for red wine. But first you need to set the water glass. It goes above the plate and a little to the right. And then you put the wine glass to the right of the water glass.

Ming: Like this?

Mrs. Riley: Exactly. Now, this little plate here is for bread. You put it above the dinner plate to the left. And this is a special knife for butter. Lay it across the top of the bread plate.

Ming: All right. What's next?

Mrs. Riley: Silverware.

Ming: Sorry?

Mrs. Riley: Silverware. Knives, forks, and spoons. There are different ones for each course. Are you serving a salad?

Ming: Yes.

Mrs. Riley: And soup?

Ming: Yes.

Mrs. Riley: OK. Take this dinner knife and put it to the right of the dinner plate. Then put the soup spoon to the right of the knife. Good. Now, to the left of the plate, first put this big fork. That's the dinner fork. And put this smaller fork to the left of that. It's for salad. OK. Now, what are you serving for dessert?

Ming: Chocolate cake.

Mrs. Riley: Then you need a dessert fork. Put it above the dinner plate, with the handle pointing to the left. And then put this small spoon, for coffee, above it, with the handle pointing to the right.

Ming: All these knives and forks! How do people know which ones to use?

Mrs. Riley: Actually it's quite simple. You always use the utensil that's on the outside, and you serve the food in the same order. So, for example, you'll serve your soup first, your salad second, your main course third, and the dessert last. See?

Ming: Yes. It's really quite logical. Thanks, Mrs. Riley. You've been a great help!

Mrs. Riley: You're welcome.

Ming: Now I just have to make sure not to burn the food!

PART 1 Conversation: Touring a Health Club

3 Listening for Main Ideas page 124

4 Listening for Details page 124

5 Listening for Stressed Words page 124

Adel: Hi, I'm Adel. I'm sure you're going to like it here. Let me show you around. Here's the weight room. We've got the newest machines, and our instructors can show you how to use them.

Peter: This is cool!

Kenji: Yeah. I really need to start lifting weights.

Adel: And here is a cardio class…

Peter: I've never tried cardio. It's just dancing, isn't it?

Adel: Not really. Actually, they're working harder than you think.

Kenji: And cardio is very good for your heart.

Adel: It sure is. But you should do it at least three times a week if you want to be in good shape.

Peter: Well, I already jog three times a week.

Adel: That's terrific.

Kenji: You also have boxing and yoga classes here, don't you?

Adel: Yes. I'll give you a schedule of classes when we finish our tour. Now here's our swimming pool.

Peter: Wow! Look at that woman in the middle lane. She's really fast, isn't she!

Adel: Oh, yeah. That's Ellen, one of our instructors.

Kenji: I'd like to take lessons from her!

Adel: You're not the only one. C'mon, I'll show you the showers and the locker room.

Adel: You know, if you want to join our gym, you ought to do it before the end of the month.

Kenji: Really? Why?

Adel: Well, because we have a special discount for students this month. Let's go to my office and I'll tell you all about it.

8 **Understanding Tag Questions**
page 127

1. **Peter:** I've never tried cardio. It's just dancing, isn't it?

   Adel: Not really.

2. **Kenji:** You also have boxing and yoga classes here, don't you?

   Adel: Yes.

3. **Peter:** Wow! Look at that woman in the middle lane. She's really fast, isn't she?

   Adel: Oh, yeah. That's Ellen, one of our instructors.

4. **Peter:** The gym is open 24 hours a day, isn't it?

   Adel: Almost. It's open from 5 A.M. to 1 A.M.

5. **Kenji:** The pool is really crowded, isn't it?

   Peter: Yeah.

6. **Adel:** You guys are students, aren't you?

   Peter and Kenji: Yes, we are.

PART 2 A Doctor's Advice: Treating an Illness

3 Listening for Main Ideas page 132

4 Taking Notes on Specific Information page 132

Doctor: Barbara, you're back again! What seems to be the trouble?

Barbara: Well, I woke up this morning with a terrible headache.

Doctor: Yes?

Barbara: And I had an upset stomach too.

I'm feeling really weak, and my whole body feels hot, and my muscles hurt. Oh, and I'm starting to get a sore throat.

Doctor: Well, your forehead feels really warm. You probably have a fever. Let me see your throat.

Barbara: Ahhhh.

Doctor: Ah-hah. It's all red and swollen. I think you've got another case of the flu. You were sick just last month, weren't you?

Barbara: Yeah, I was.

Doctor: Are you taking good care of yourself?

Barbara: What do you mean?

Doctor: Well, do you eat right, and do you get enough sleep?

Barbara: Well, right now I'm studying for some tests and I'm very tired. I've been drinking a lot of coffee and eating pizza and hamburgers.

Doctor: You should stop drinking coffee and eat lots of fruits and vegetables. I want you to take two aspirin four times a day, drink a lot of juice, and get plenty of rest. If your throat doesn't get better in a week, I want you to call me, OK?

Barbara: So I don't need a prescription, do I?

Doctor: Not yet. Well, try to take care of yourself, and don't work too hard.

PART 3 Strategies for Better Listening and Speaking

Focus on Testing: Using Context Clues page 135

Part 1: Conversation 1

Man: Hello, may I take your order?

Woman: Yes, I'd like a salad with low-fat cottage cheese, no dressing, please. And one slice of bread, no butter.

Man: Anything to drink?

Woman: Do you have unsweetened iced tea?

Man: Yes, we do. Will that be all, Miss?

Woman: Yes... oh, wait! For dessert I'll have a piece of chocolate cake with ice cream.

Question 1:
What's surprising about the woman's order?

Man: You know, before you ordered that cake, I thought you were on a diet.

Conversation 2

Woman: So that was a good workout, wasn't it?

Man: Yeah. Let's see... what did we do? We ran three miles, we played two sets of tennis, and we did 50 sit-ups.

Woman: Yeah. I want to get a nice cold bottle of water from the vending machine.

Man: And I want to get a bag of potato chips.

Question 2:
What's surprising about what the man says?

Woman: You know, you take such good care of yourself and get so much exercise. I really don't understand why you eat junk like potato chips.

Conversation 3

Woman: Why did you wake me up?

Man: You were sleeping quite awhile. I think you should cover up and get into the shade.

Woman: You think so? I really want to get a good tan.

Man: Well, you already look a bit red to me.

Woman: Don't worry. I do this every summer at the beach.

Question 3:
What's surprising about what the woman says?

Man: You shouldn't lie in the sun so long without protection. You're going to get a *terrible* sunburn.

Conversation 4

Man: Hi, Andrea. How're you doing?

Woman: I am so stressed out! I can't eat, I can't sleep. I feel like I'm going crazy!

Man: Why? What's the problem?

Woman: I've got so many things to do. You know, school, my job, housework, sports—there just isn't enough time for everything.

Man: You really ought to take a vacation. Maybe go to Hawaii for a week.

Woman: Oh, I don't want to do that.

Man: Why not?

Woman: It's so boring there. There's nothing to do.

Question 4:
What's surprising about what Andrea said?

Man: I don't get it. You're complaining about how stressed out you are, but you don't even want some time to relax!

Part 2: Conversation 1

A: So Nancy went into the hospital last night?

B: That's right, and her husband is waiting for the news right now.

A: Is this her first?

B: Yes, so they're both very nervous. Especially Steve.

A: When can Nancy come home?

B: If all goes well, they'll both be home in a couple of days. It's exciting, isn't it?

Question 1: *The situation is...*

A: Yes, having your first baby is always very special.

Conversation 2

A: These carrots are organic.

B: What about your eggs? Are they fresh?

A: Of course. All our eggs come from local farms daily.

B: You sell vitamins, don't you?

A: Yes, they're right next to the nuts over there.

B: Your stuff looks great, but it's a little expensive.

A: Well, we sell only the best.

Question 2: *The speakers are in a...*

B: Well, I guess this is the best health food store in town.

PART 4 Real-World Tasks: Talking to Health Care Professionals

❶ Taking Notes on Phone Conversations page 138

Conversation 1

A: University Dental Clinic. May I help you?

B: Yes, I'd like to make an appointment.

A: Do you have a problem, or is it just for a checkup?

B: I think I've broken a tooth.

A: Well, can you come in tomorrow morning?

B: No, but how about after lunch?

A: Well, let me see… Dr. Jones can probably take you at around two o'clock. How's that?

B: That's great. Where is your office?

A: We're at 532 Western Avenue. That's near Third Street.

B: OK. I'll see you tomorrow at two.

Conversation 2

A: Drugs R Us. May I help you?

B: Yes, I'd like to know if my prescription is ready.

A: What's the name, please?

B: Ellen Beattie.

A: Spell that, please.

B: B-E-A-T-T-I-E.

A: Oh, yes, here it is. It comes to $14.95.

B: Are there any special instructions?

A: Well, let me see. Take the pills every six hours with food. But don't worry. The instructions are also on the bottle.

B: OK. How late can I pick it up?

A: Today we're open until five o'clock.

B: All right. Thanks a lot. I'll be in later.

Conversation 3

A: Family Medicine.

B: Hi, Sherry. This is Penny Berkowitz.

A: Hi. You're bringing your baby in this afternoon, aren't you?

B: Well, our car broke down. So I'd like to change our appointment with Dr. Stork, if that's OK.

A: Sure. What's a good time for you?

B: Can I come in on Monday?

A: How about ten o'clock?

B: Fine.

A: OK. We'll see you then.

B: Oh, while we're on the phone, my husband needs a checkup. Can you take him one evening next week?

A: I think so. What about Tuesday at six o'clock with Dr. Miller?

B: That's perfect. Thanks. Bye-bye.

CHAPTER **8** **Entertainment and the Media**

PART 1 Conversation: Watching TV

❸ Listening for Main Ideas page 145

❹ Listening for Details page 146

❺ Listening for Stressed Words page 146

Ming: Hey, listen to this. The average American watches four hours of TV a day.

Jack: A day? You're joking.

Ming: No, it says so right here in this newspaper. Hmm, I guess you're an average American, Jack. You always have your TV on.

Jack: Come on. Are you saying I'm a couch potato?

Ming: Yeah. I really think watching TV is a waste of time.

Jack: Oh, come on. Some programs are bad, like those soap operas. But what about sports or the news? You watch those sometimes, don't you?

Ming: Well, actually, for the news, I prefer the newspaper. Or the Internet.

Jack: Why?

Ming: First, because they give you a lot more information. And I can read them any time I want. Plus, I hate all the commercials.

Jack: I know what you mean. That's why, when the commercials come on, I just turn down the volume or change channels.

Ming: Yeah, I noticed that. Channel surfing drives me crazy.

Jack: OK, next time you come over, I'll let you have the remote control.

Ming: Oh, that's so sweet. But I have a better idea. Next time I come over, let's just turn the TV off.

7 Listening for Reductions page 147

A: Are you calling the movie theater?

B: Uh-huh. Don't you want to go to the movies tonight?

A: To tell you the truth, I'm pretty tired. But we can go to an early show. Do you know what you want to see?

B: Not really. I'll let you choose. *Batman III* is playing at eight and James Bond is at ten.

A: Let's see *Batman III*. I'm tired now and by ten o'clock I'm going to be dead.

PART 2 New Report: An Airplane Crash

3 Listening for Main Ideas page 152

4 Listening for Specific Information page 152

Radio Announcer: Good evening. Our top story tonight: about an hour ago, a small airplane carrying six people landed safely in traffic on Highway 1. Two of the passengers received back injuries, and one of the passengers suffered a broken leg. Here's reporter Laura Jones at the scene of the crash.

Reporter: Good evening, Mark. I'm standing here on Highway 1 with two drivers who almost hit the plane as it landed. Could you tell me what you thought as you watched the plane coming down?

Witness 1: Well, at first I wasn't scared. But then I saw it was flying very low. So I drove to the side of the road in a hurry.

Reporter: And you, sir?

Witness 2: I almost didn't see the plane at all. It happened so fast. When I finally heard the plane's engine, I knew something was wrong. And then I hit my brakes. Phew… it was really close. I'm still shaking.

Reporter: Fortunately, no one on the ground was hurt, but the plane blocked traffic for over an hour. Officer John McNamara of the local highway police thinks the plane ran out of gasoline. A complete investigation will begin tomorrow. Back to you, Mark.

PART 3 Strategies for Better Listening and Speaking

Focus on Testing: Using Context Clues page 154

Commercial 1

Announcer:
Looking for a healthy start and a delicious flavor? Time to go to work, but no time to cook a healthy breakfast? Start your morning right with a bowl of *Flakos*!

Question 1: *What are Flakos?*

Anncr: They're my favorite cereal, and they provide all the energy I need for the morning.

Commercial 2

A: Hello?

B: Hi, Marge. Are you asleep?

A: Not anymore. Who is this?

B: It's Bill. I'm on vacation in California.

A: Bill, it's 12 o'clock midnight.

B: Yeah, but I have some good news! I'm calling for free! I get 5,000 free night-time minutes on this new calling plan. And I got a great new camera phone!

Question 2: *This is an ad for a...*

Anncr: SureCell—the cell phone company that saves you money all day—and all night!

Commercial 3

Hi! This is Tex Lewis. I'll do anything to sell you one of these fine beauties. Lookie here. We've got a 2005 two-door sedan here, automatic, with low mileage. This baby is clean; got new tires, GPS system, side airbags, the whole works. Take a test drive today. And it can be yours for just $16,000, or $500 per month. Come in and check it out. See you soon.

Question 3: *This is an ad for...*

Anncr: Tex's Used Cars. Quality cars for less.

Commercial 4

Male: Honey, make me a sandwich.

Female: Henry! It's midnight. I'm tired.

Male: Honey, what's on TV?

Female: I don't know. It's two o'clock in the morning.

Male: Honey, can I have some breakfast?

Female: Henry, it's four o'clock in the morning. Why don't you take some Dreamease?

Question 4: *Dreamease is a...*

Anncr: Dreamease, the sleeping pill that helps you get the rest you need.

Commercial 5

Man: Daisy, you must tell me everything. You believe me, don't you?

Woman: I can't, Rob. I just can't.

Man: Don't treat me this way, Daisy. I know you love me. And I love you, too.

Woman: I know. But, but I promised. And I can't break a promise.

Anncr: Her secret can destroy a life. Will she tell it? Find out this Monday at nine on KNXT.

Question 5: *This is an ad for a...*

Anncr: *Daisy,* the most popular drama on television.

PART 4   Real-World Tasks: Talking About TV Shows

2 **Discussing a Program Guide** page 156

Jennifer: What's on TV tonight?

Raul: Let me check the TV guide. What time is it now?

Jennifer: It's almost seven-thirty.

Raul: There are probably some game shows on.

Jennifer: Yeah, I think *Who Wants to Be a Millionaire?* is on Channel 7 at seven o'clock.

Raul: *Who Wants to Be a Millionaire?* I'm a little tired of that one.

Jennifer: OK. See if there're any good movies on.

Raul: Well, there are three movies on at eight o'clock.

Jennifer: Which ones are they?

Raul: There's *Shanghai Knights* on Channel 13—you know, the comedy with Jackie Chan.

Jennifer: I've already seen it.

Raul: Then on Channel 11 there's *The Matrix.* But you don't like science fiction, right?

Jennifer: Ugh. I hate sci-fi.

Raul: And then there's the horror movie *Scream*... that's on Channel 20.

Jennifer: Oh, wait—what's tonight? Wednesday? My favorite sitcom is on at eight o'clock!

Raul: At eight? You must be kidding—you don't want to watch *Friends* again! Channel 53 should take it off, it's so old.

Jennifer: I don't care. *Friends* is still the funniest.

Jennifer: Come on, let's make a decision.

Raul: OK. We can watch your sitcom at eight if you let me watch basketball at nine on Channel 25.

Jennifer: Basketball? But you played basketball all afternoon!

Raul: But it's the NBA finals!

Jennifer: Fine. But I want to catch the news at 8:30. I want to know about the president's trip to Asia.

Raul: Yeah, me too. I'm sure CNN on Channel 24 will have a good report.

Jennifer: Yeah. I guess we're all set. I'll go make some popcorn.

CHAPTER **9** **Social Life**

PART 1 Conversation: Making a Date

3 **Listening for Main Ideas** page 164

4 **Listening for Details** page 164

5 **Listening for Stressed Words** page 164

Yolanda: Ming, look! I can't believe it! It's Dan. Hey, Dan! How are you?

Dan: Yolanda? Ming? Wow! I haven't seen you guys since graduation night!

Ming: I know. You look great!

Dan: Thanks. So do you!

Ming: So what have you been up to?

Dan: Well, I go to Faber College.

Yolanda: Really? Do you like it?

Dan: Yeah, so far. But I've been studying really hard.

Ming: Sure you have…

Yolanda: So, what's your major?

Dan: It's computer science.

Ming: Ah-h-h. That makes sense. You always were good at math and science.

Dan: Thanks. Anyway, what have you guys been up to?

Ming: Well, I'm a sales rep for a publishing company.

Dan: No kidding! How do you like that?

Ming: Oh, I love it! I'm on the road a lot, but I get to meet some interesting people.

Dan: That's terrific. And how about you, Yolanda?

Yolanda: I'm studying pre-med at State College.

Dan: Wow—you can be my doctor! You always were good at science too. Well, it was great seeing you both. Let's keep in touch from now on. Email me sometime. Here's my address.

8 **Matching Statements and Responses** page 167

1. My sister just had triplets.
2. Guess what? I'm getting married next month.
3. Would you like a job for a dollar an hour?
4. I've been dancing a lot, and I've finally learned the tango.
5. Someone hit my car yesterday. It's going to cost $1,000 to repair.
6. I met the president of the United States yesterday.
7. My sister likes to eat peanut butter and banana sandwiches.
8. I locked the keys in the car.

PART 2 Conversation: Arranging a Match

2 **Listening for Main Ideas** page 168

3 **Taking Notes on Specific Information** page 169

Tanya: Listen, Meena, a friend is coming

to town next week. He's great looking, and I think you might enjoy going on a date. Would you like to meet him?

Meena: No thanks, Tanya. You know how traditional my family is. Dating just isn't part of our culture. In fact, I'm not supposed to go out with guys at all before marriage.

Tanya: Hmm, I see. How are you going to meet a partner, or a husband?

Meena: Oh, my family's always looking for the right kind of person. Or they might even take me to a professional matchmaker.

Tanya: Interesting… So what makes a good match?

Meena: Well, he's got to be from a good family from my parents' point of view. And he has to share our religious beliefs.

Tanya: That's just what my mother says. And…?

Meena: He should be honest and hardworking, be a strong leader, but be kind.

Tanya: Sounds good to me. But what if you don't love the guy your family wants you to be with?

Meena: You know, my parents would never force me to marry someone I really couldn't accept… But we believe love is something that takes time— it can grow in the right situation.

Tanya: I think I understand…

Meena: Maybe it doesn't sound very romantic. But our family life is really strong, and all my relatives seem pretty satisfied with their marriages.

Tanya: I wish I could say the same…

Focus on Testing: Using Context Clues page 174

Conversation 1

Man: So how long have you lived here?

Woman: I've lived here all my life. I really love it here.

Man: It seems nice, but I've been so busy with my new job and moving in to my new apartment that I haven't done any sightseeing yet. Are you free on Saturday afternoon? Maybe you could show me around a little.

Question 1: *Which of these sentences is true?*

Woman: Sure. Tell me, how long have you been in town?

Man: Only about three weeks.

Conversation 2

Woman: So, are you glad you left?

Man: Very glad. My salary wasn't great, as you know, and the manager was a pain in the neck.

Woman: He still is. Every day I hate going to work. But I don't know if I could find a better job.

Man: Why don't you start looking around? You might get lucky like me.

Question 2: *Which of these sentences is true?*

Man: I really enjoyed working with you, of course. I just didn't like the boss.

Conversation 3

Man: I've really enjoyed talking with you. Would you like to have lunch together sometime?

Woman: Thanks, you're very kind. But, well, uh, it's difficult for me to get away from work. I'm very busy.

Man: Well, how about dinner?

Woman: I'm usually too tired to go out after work.

Man: Can I call you over the weekend?

Woman: Well, this weekend my friend is coming from Miami, and I'll probably be out most of the time.

Man: How about next weekend?

Question 3: *Which of these sentences is true?*

Woman: Actually, I have a boyfriend, so I really can't go out with you.

Conversation 4

Man: Where's Tony?

Woman: I think he took his bike out to get some soda.

Man: Really? Do you think he can see out there? I mean it's pitch dark!

Woman: I don't know. I'm sure he's fine. It's only been about an hour.

Question 4: *Which of these sentences is true?*

Man: One hour! The store is just five minutes from here. I hope he's OK.

Conversation 5

Woman: Where were you? I waited forty-five minutes before I left for the party.

Man: I thought you were going to pick me up. I had to take a taxi.

Woman: Wait a minute. You said you wanted to leave your car at my house.

Man: That's not what I said. I said I wanted to leave my car *at home*.

Question 5: *Which of these sentences is true?*

Woman: Listen, I'm sorry. Let's not fight over this misunderstanding, OK?

PART 4 Real-World Tasks: Making Social Plans

3 **Taking Notes** page 178

Call 1

Hello. This is the Fox Theater, located in the Town and Country Shopping Center. Today we're proud to present Nicole Kidman in the thrilling sci-fi film, *Invasion*. Show times for Saturday are two, six, and ten o'clock. Tickets are $10 and $8.50 for students, senior citizens, and children under 12. For more information, please hang up and call 555-0183. See you at the movies!

Call 2

Manager: Hello. Blue Note Jazz and Supper Club.

Ming: Hi. I'd like some information.

Manager: Sure, what would you like to know?

Ming: First, is there any live music tonight?

Manager: Yes, we have a terrific Brazilian singer named Bebel Gilberto. There are shows at nine and eleven.

Ming: How much is the show?

Manager: We have a $20 cover charge. But if you come for dinner, the show is free.

Ming: What's your menu like?

Manager: Our specialty is Italian food, but we serve salads and hamburgers too.

Ming: Fine. I'd like to make a reservation for two for dinner at eight, and we'll stay for the nine o'clock show. My last name's Lee—that's L-E-E.

Manager: Very good Ms. Lee, we'll see you at eight.

Call 3

You have reached the information line for Gallery Shibuya, which features live rock music nightly. The gallery is proud to present *Buffalo Daughter*, now through August 6. For show times, press 1. For directions to Gallery Shibuya, press 2. For ticket information and ticket orders, press 3.

Clerk: Hi, this is Sherry speaking. Can I help you?

Ming: Yes, uh, do you still have tickets for the August 4th *Buffalo Daughter* show?

Clerk: How many tickets?

Ming: Two.

Clerk: I'll check.

Clerk: Yes, we have tickets for $20.

Ming: Is there a special price for students?

Clerk: Yes, student tickets are $8.50.

Ming: OK, that's good.

Clerk: All right, two student tickets at $8.50 each, that's $17. There is also a service charge of $1 per ticket, so your total comes to $19. And how would you like to pay for your tickets?

Ming: Can you hold them for me for ten minutes—I'm just a block away from you?

Clerk: I can do that—and then there's no service charge. May I have your full name please?

Ming: Ming Lee.

Clerk: Ming—M-I-N-G?

Ming: Right.

Clerk: And we need your phone number please, Ms. Lee?

Ming: 310-555-0176.

Clerk: OK, so we'll see you soon, all right? And remember to bring your student ID with you, for the student price.

Ming: Thank you very much.

Clerk: You're welcome. Bye-bye.

Ming: Bye.

CHAPTER **10** **Sports**

PART 1 Conversation: Explaining a Sport

3 Listening for Main Ideas page 183

4 Listening for Details page 184

5 Listening for Stressed Words page 184

Ming: OK guys. Let's warm up and stretch. We've got to work on balance and flexibility.

Peter: So Ming. When did you get into this karate stuff?

Kenji: Karate's Japanese. Ming's showing us Tae Kwan Do, and it's Korean.

Peter: Cool. So, what's the difference?

Ming: Tae Kwan Do uses hundreds of different kicking moves. But karate... well, Kenji, it sounds like you know something about karate.

Kenji: Yeah—karate uses more punches and blocks, too. Maybe you've seen guys break wooden boards with punches. You know, like... I learned that when I was in school.

Peter: That's great. I wish I could do that. So, Ming, why did you get into Tae Kwan Do?

Ming: I had a Korean friend in middle school and he said it could help me get in shape and build my confidence. So I tried it, and I really liked it.

Peter: It looks like you succeeded.

Ming: Well, I'm still working on it. I've really improved my speed and power. It also helps you focus—you'll see.

Peter: Awesome! Let's get started.

8 Listening for Reductions page 186

Jane: Hi Helen. Are you going out?

Helen: Yeah, I'm going to the football game. My brother's playing and I thought I'd watch him. Do you want to come?

Jane: I really can't... I have to study. But can you do me a favor?

Helen: OK.

Jane: Could you get me tickets for the girls' soccer game next Saturday? My cousin Sue just made the team.

Helen: Sure—that's so cool. What's her position?

Jane: I'm not sure—I'm going to call her, and I can ask her, if you want.

Helen: You don't have to—just wish her luck.

PART 2 Speech: A Female Wrestler

3 Taking Notes on Main Ideas page 189

5 Listening for Specific Information page 190

Hi, my name is Terri Whitmore. I'm 21 years old, I major in psychology, I have a boyfriend, and I love movies and shopping and cats. Yeah, most people think I'm a typical college student. That's until they find out that I'm a champion wrestler. Then of course they're surprised because in most parts of the United States and the world, the idea of women's wrestling is still new. What people don't know is that women's wrestling is growing very quickly, especially since the 2004 Olympics. That's when women's wrestling was finally included as an Olympic sport. Imagine: the sport of wrestling is one of the oldest in history, but women wrestlers couldn't compete until recently.

Anyway, people always ask me, "Why did you choose wrestling?" Well, to me it was natural. I became interested when I was eight because my brothers were on wrestling teams. They let me participate, and I did very well. I mean I won a lot of matches and beat most of the guys. But when I turned 12, they didn't want me on the team anymore just because I was a girl. When I went to college, I started to wrestle again, this time on girls' teams.

Another thing people ask is about the rules. Are they the same as for men? Sure. Basically, the main goal in wrestling is to pin your opponent. That means you try to hold their shoulders to the floor for about one-half second. If you do that, you win right away. But there are other ways to win a match, too. You can score points; I mean points for different moves and holds. The wrestler with the most points is the winner. But you need at least three more points than the other guy. If not, then you go into overtime.

Oh, and then there are all kinds of rules about the parts of the body. You know, the parts that are OK to touch or hold, and things like that. And also, it's important to know that we compete against wrestlers in the same weight group.

Anyway, I'm really glad I chose wrestling. I like competing as an individual. In team sports, you can always blame someone else for not scoring a goal, or not catching a ball. But my success or my failure depends only on me, not on a teammate. Sure, it's a lot of pressure, but it's made me stronger and more confident.

PART 3 Strategies for Better Listening and Speaking

Focus on Testing: Using Context Clues page 192

1. You can do this sport all year: outside in the summer and inside in the winter. You don't need any special equipment, just a bathing suit. You can do it by yourself, but you can't do it without water.

2. This sport looks like two people are fighting. They wear gloves and special protection for their teeth and sometimes for their heads. Usually men do this sport. But in the past few years, women have been participating in this sport, too.

3. This sport is not very old. It started as just a fun activity for young people who wanted to try something different from skiing. It's kind of a mix between surfing and skiing. Sometimes it's called an extreme sport, but in 1998 it became part of the Winter Olympics. Some people think this sport will be more popular than skiing in the future.

4. This sport is thousands of years old. Today it's one of the most popular Olympic events because it's very beautiful to watch. Men and women need to have great flexibility, balance, and strength as they perform exercises on the floor or on special equipment.

5. This sport is a game between two teams of nine or ten players. One player throws the ball to another, who tries to hit it with a stick as far as possible. Other players use gloves to catch the ball. This sport is especially popular in North America and Japan.

PART 4 Real-World Tasks: Following Sports News

3 Sports News on the Radio page 196

Announcer Bill: And now, to Yao Lam and Kristin Fox for Faber College Weekend Sports!

Kristin: Thanks, Bill. Well, it was a busy weekend in sports, wasn't it Yao?

Yao: Sure was, Kristin. Well, Faber College men's basketball lost a big game to State College, 76 to 72.

Kristin: Yeah, it was too bad—it was really close down to the last few seconds… On the other hand, our *women's* basketball team won their game easily. They beat Hamilton College 61 to 43.

Yao: They get stronger every game. Now turning to volleyball, the women got a rest this weekend, but the men's team played down at Washington Junior College, and they were just *unbeatable*!

Kristin: That's right—they won all three games: 21 to 15, 21 to 18, and 21 to 12. In the state college tennis tournament, we can be very proud of our own Johnson sisters.

Yao: Yeah, the twins are playing really well. Mary Johnson won her match without any trouble: 6–3, 6–2. It took her just half an hour to finish her opponent, Tina Lewis.

Kristin: Her sister, Susan Johnson, had to work a little harder, but also was a winner against her rival, Lisa Kim. The scores for the sets were 6–4, 4–6, 7–5. It was the longest match of the day.

Yao: And finally, our women's soccer team is playing some matches on a tour down in Brazil.

Kristin: I wish I was down there reporting on that!

Yao: Me too. I understand they just finished their first game, and they almost beat the girls from College Club Rio.

Kristin: Really, what was the score?

Yao: Actually, it was a 3–3 tie—so no losers… well that's it for Weekend Sports.

Kristen and Yao: Go Faber!!

Vocabulary Index

Chapter 7

aspirin
boxing
cardio
discount
eat right
fever
headache
health club
in good/bad shape
jog
lane
lift weights
locker room
ought to
prescription
rest
show (someone) around
sore throat
swim
swollen
upset stomach
weak
yoga

Chapter 8

average week
block
change channels
channel surf
couch potato
hurt
injury
land
passenger
remote control
run out of
top story
turn down the volume
turn on the TV
turn the TV off
the TV
waste of time

Chapter 9

be up to
box office
cover charge
good at
graduation
keep in touch
live music
make a reservation
make sense
on the road
pre-med
sales rep
sci-fi movie
service charge
show times
terrific
vacancy

Chapter 10

balance
beat
close
compete
confidence
flexibility
focus
get in shape
get into
individual
It was a close game.
It was a tie!
lose
loser
match
opponent
overtime
rival
score
set
stretch
tennis match
tie
warm up
What was the score?
win
winner